Awakening Love

Awakening Love

*How to Love Your
Neighbor as Yourself*

Gina Lake

Endless Satsang Foundation

www.RadicalHappiness.com

Cover art: © Daniel B. Holeman
http://www.AwakenVisions.com

ISBN: 979-8627324388

Copyright © 2020 by Gina Lake

All rights reserved. No part of this book may be used or reproduced by any means, graphic, electronic, or mechanical, including photocopying, recording, taping, or by any information storage retrieval system without the written permission of the publisher except in the case of brief quotations embodied in critical articles and reviews.

Contents

Preface — vii
Introduction — xiii

Chapter 1: Loving Yourself — 1

Chapter 2: Loving Your Neighbor — 21

Chapter 3: The Golden Rule — 35

Chapter 4: It Is More Blessed to Give Than to Receive — 51

Chapter 5: Love God with All Your Heart — 65

Chapter 6: As You Sow, so Shall You Reap — 77

Chapter 7: The Way and the Truth and the Life — 91

Chapter 8: As a Man Thinketh, so Is He — 107

Chapter 9: Conclusion — 125

About the Author — 129
An Excerpt from *Choosing Love* — 131

Preface

Before Jesus introduces this book himself in the Introduction that follows, I'd like to set the stage for this book and explain how it and the others I've received from Jesus have been written. They were given to me word for word through a kind of dictation that is heard very clearly in my head and is distinct from my own thoughts.

This process is called conscious channeling, since I am conscious and not in an altered state when I'm receiving these words. I can even be moving around and still hear the words, as long as my mind is silent. I've received ten other books from Jesus this way, which have required no organizing and only light editing on my part.

When I'm writing a book, it's as if Jesus is sitting beside me dictating to me. I feel his presence, and his words have a distinct tonality and feel to them, an energy, reflective of the kindness, gentleness, and strength of the one we have known as Jesus the Christ.

This type of channeling is not that rare. Both saints and more ordinary people have had this gift. In Catholicism, it is called interior locution. St. Teresa of Avila wrote about it in her sixteenth century book *The Interior Castle*.

However, there are many misconceptions about channeling, particularly on the part of fundamentalist Christians, who have been told that channeling is "of the

Devil." They support this claim with a few passages from the Old Testament, which are not upheld in the New Testament.

The irony is that many of the revelations received by the prophets and others in the Scriptures were received this way or clairvoyantly, through visions. Furthermore, many Christians claim that God or Jesus speaks directly to them, or they attribute such words to the Holy Spirit, which is Christianity's way of acknowledging that God speaks to us and guides us internally. Paranormal events, such as hearing the voice of God or some other entity and seeing visions, abound in the Bible, and such events are not limited to ancient times. Throughout history, these communications have sustained and inspired humanity and been responsible for some of our most important inventions.

That doesn't mean we shouldn't be discerning; not all other-dimensional communications are from trustworthy sources. But we don't need to declare that all channeling is evil. In 1 John 4:1, we are told: "Do not believe every spirit, but test the spirits to see whether they are from God." This implies that some are from God. And in 1 Thessalonians 5:21, we are told to "test all things and hold on to what is good." How do we test these things? Jesus offered this guideline: "By their fruits, you will know them." We will know what is true and not true by the fruits of our beliefs. The Truth bears good results; the false does not.

Jesus, himself, received information and guidance from other dimensions through both intuition and voices. He knew the purpose of his life and he knew his destiny—he knew how he would die. He knew things that others didn't. But he is not the only one this can be said of. And nowhere in the Bible did Jesus discourage people from connecting with nonphysical guiding forces. For example, in Matthew 17, Jesus was said to have spoken to Moses and Elijah, who died long before. This was such a transformative moment for Jesus that it is called the transfiguration by the Catholic church and celebrated with a holy day.

Jesus had a personal connection to God, and he encouraged each of us to connect with God: "Ask and it will be given to you; seek and you will find; knock and the door will be opened to you." Jesus did not set himself up as a mediator between us and God; human beings did. Jesus was an opponent of the hierarchical orthodoxy of the time and railed against their shallowness and hypocrisy.

When Jesus said, "I am the Way and the Truth and the Life. No one comes to the Father but through me," Jesus was speaking of himself as a representative of love. What he was saying was that *love* is the Way, the Truth, and the Life, and no one comes to God except through love, through what Jesus taught.

The distortion of this quote has been very divisive. It has allowed Christianity to assume exclusivity and superiority. This quote was used to set Jesus up as the one, true emissary—son—of God, which is untrue. This belief, held by so many Christians, has been devastating to peace and unity on this planet. This quote has been used to justify judging, alienating, and even persecuting those who hold other beliefs. This was not Jesus's way. This is an example of how the ego has corrupted Christianity and how the ego corrupts religion in general.

Jesus was available to everyone, regardless of someone's beliefs and even behavior. This inclusiveness was one of the things that made Jesus so remarkable. He embraced even sinners and those who were cast out of society. He told us to love everyone, not just those who are like us, related to us, or easy to love.

In my books, Jesus has repeatedly invited people to call upon him. He wants them to know that he is with everyone who is sincerely devoted to him and his message of love, regardless of their religious beliefs. The proof of his availability is that his presence is felt by everyone who loves him and calls upon him, in churches or wherever they are.

Humanity is very special to Jesus, and he is very special to humanity, although Jesus is not the only one guiding and shoring up humanity. Jesus exists today in a higher dimension along with others who are lovingly and compassionately guiding and supporting humanity. And Jesus continues to inspire many with his teachings, through the books he dictates and in private contemplation and meditation.

Why would this not be so, when it is possible to do this? If Jesus still exists, and he does, he would surely care enough about humanity to continue to do what he could to uplift humanity. And so, he does.

The presence of loving, wise, nonphysical beings, such as Jesus, is a great blessing and gift that humanity has been given, without which we would be quite lost. Whether you call these nonphysical beings God or angels or Ascended Masters or spirit guides, they are a very real phenomenon.

Jesus's message two thousand years ago and now is that we, too, are essentially divine, not sinners, although we struggle with having an ego. Jesus was an example of what we all can be, a model of what is possible for every human being, a model of a loving human being. His message was that we, too, can be Christed—enlightened—as he was. If this were not so, why would he even try to teach us to be like him? We are all sons and daughters of God. Unfortunately, Christians misunderstood who Jesus was.

Is this so blasphemous to suggest that human beings might have misunderstood who Jesus was and even misunderstood his message at times? Christianity was created by people, and people misunderstand things all the time, especially deep and esoteric things, and people were quite primitive and uneducated when the Bible was written and Christianity was founded.

Ever since Jesus walked the earth, people have misunderstood him and his teachings, and Christianity has perpetuated some of these misunderstandings. Isn't that obvious? If Christianity had gotten it entirely right, wouldn't we be living more as Jesus taught than we are, two thousand years later? If Christianity had gotten it entirely right, I doubt that we would have engaged in the Crusades or the Inquisition or any other religious war. If we had really understood what he was teaching, wouldn't we have put an end to war by now? Wouldn't we have learned to get along with those whose beliefs are different from ours? Wouldn't we have stopped judging?

Instead, Christianity and other religions have contributed to perpetuating war, persecution, conflict, and judgment. This is not to deny the good fostered by Christianity or any other religion, but to point out that Christianity is flawed. It is fallible, and it is fallible because people created it. Not everything it claims as Truth is the truth.

Jesus urged us to be peaceful, to love others, and not to judge. His teachings were not separative but sought to unite people. Jesus did not establish a religion. Religions were created by people. Jesus, Buddha, and other enlightened human beings brought the Truth to humanity, and then humanity misunderstood or distorted much of their teachings. There is no one, true religion; there is only Truth.

Somewhere, we took a wrong turn. We haven't stayed true to the principles of love and peace that Jesus taught. We believed things that were counter to love, counter to peace, counter to Jesus's teachings. Some of those beliefs even became doctrine. We mistook faith to mean faith in doctrine rather than faith in the existence and goodness of God. We settled for a religion of rules rather than one that connected us to the depths of our being.

We fell prey to dogma, rigid rules, guilt, shame, fear, the belief in punishment, and the doctrine of sin and unworthiness. Many are being held hostage to dogma by the fear of Hell and damnation. But Jesus did not attract and hold the masses with fear, nor should Christianity. He attracted the masses because he was speaking Truth, and they knew the Truth when they heard it.

Fortunately, the core teachings of Jesus have been preserved, and these teachings are primarily about love, which is what this book is about. In this and my other channeled books, Jesus offers us the teachings he presented two thousand years ago and the ones he would present if he were alive today, which are essentially the same. These teachings provide the solutions that our troubled world needs, if only we have "ears to hear."

This book is a little different from the others I've written in that it will explore what Jesus meant by some of the quotes attributed to him, particularly about love. In this way, we will thoroughly explore the topic of love: what love is, how to love, why it's difficult to love, and what love in today's world looks like.

I hope you'll be able to set aside any preconceptions and expectations around Jesus speaking to us in this way and just allow the words to touch your heart and transform your mind.

Let the fruits of these teachings inform you of their truth. The truth of these words will be self-evident in your life when you put them to the test. So now, I will step aside so that you can experience, more directly, the one who was and is known as Jesus Christ, as he speaks to us about love.

Gina Lake
April, 2020

Introduction

This is the one you have known as Jesus the Christ. In this book, I offer my most important teachings: teachings about love. Why I've been remembered and why some have come to see me as God is simply because I spoke the Truth. The Truth is that powerful and that resonant within you. In your heart of hearts, you know the Truth, and you know the Truth will set you free. You know there is Truth and that it is worth seeking. And some of you are ready to discover it once and for all.

This Truth is something that every person knows. This truth is that love is the answer to every question and to how to behave. What should I do? Love. How do I proceed? Lovingly. What do I do about…? Accept the situation with love and compassion and peacefully wait for guidance to appear. How can I become happy? Love. How can I find a partner? Love. How can I get along with my neighbor, my boss, my enemy? Love. If you answer any of these questions any other way, you won't be happy, you will struggle, you will have problems, you will suffer, you will lack support from others. It is that simple.

And yet, love seems to be a very difficult thing to do. Why is that, and how can this be overcome? That is what this book is about. My hope is to awaken the love within you, which is what you honor about me. I am but a model of what a human being can be and is meant to be.

You are meant to be loving, happy, and at peace. This is possible, and the way to be this is to know this and then cultivate the love that is within you. Cultivate means create conditions under which love can flower. Nourish and nurture love. Yes, it takes effort to be loving, but the rewards are great. Although love needs cultivation, once it has sprouted, it grows on its own because, as a spark of God, it is your nature to love.

This book is what I would teach about love if I were walking among you today. It takes its organization from particular quotes of mine and others from the Bible, which have come down through time. These are quotes that represent what I taught two thousand years ago. Not all of the things I purportedly said that are recorded in the Bible are accurate, but the quotes this book is built upon are the core teachings I gave then and I offer you today. If they are adhered to, they will change your life and change your world.

Jesus, dictated to Gina Lake
April, 2020

Chapter 1

Loving Yourself

The essence of my teaching when I walked the earth and now is love. The key instruction and the summation of the Commandments is to love. What does it mean to love? What does love look like? It looks like this: "Love your neighbor as yourself" and "Do unto others as you would have them do unto you." These two instructions contain the essence of my teachings and the secret to being happy and flourishing as an individual and as a society.

The first part of this, "Love your neighbor as yourself," is a real challenge for some. "What if I don't love myself? How do I love myself?" It isn't a given that you love yourself, so we must start there. What does it mean to love yourself, and how do you love yourself?

Sometimes you love yourself by eating cookies or buying yourself a present. Or you might try to improve yourself to become more loveable. If more people love you, you think, then maybe you'll love yourself. Too often, loving yourself means either indulging yourself or doing something to try to get others to love you. But that's not what I'm talking about. These are the ego's solutions to not loving yourself.

So, let's talk about the ego for a moment, since the ego is the reason that people don't love themselves. The ego is the conditioned self and the sense of yourself as an individual, apart from others. It is reflected in the voice in your head, especially in all the thoughts that begin with "I." The ego is the sense of *me, who I am, who I want to be, who I was in the past, who I will be, what I want and don't want,* and *what I like and don't like.* The ego is made up of all the beliefs you have about yourself and what you believe others believe about you.

The ego is not actually real but only a sense of self built on a set of beliefs about who you are. This set of beliefs is not who you are, nor do these beliefs accurately reflect who you are, which is why the sense of self created by the ego is called the false self, as opposed to the true self, the divine self.

The ego wouldn't be a problem in terms of loving yourself if the beliefs associated with the ego and the false self were not so negative, limiting, and untrue. The problem is that the ego and the false self it creates is an unhappy self because, at its core, it feels fearful, lacking, inadequate, vulnerable, and not good enough. What's worse is that these feelings cause you to be unkind to others, which makes you feel even worse about yourself.

That's why you may not love yourself and why you may have difficulty loving others: You believe the beliefs that are part of your egoic programming. You believe you are this negative, unhappy self, and believing this causes you to function poorly and behave badly toward others. Since everyone has a similar ego and conditioning, all of humanity suffers similarly.

The truth, however, is that you are a divine being, a spiritual being, an extension of God, who is temporarily playing at being human and who *has* an ego but is not the ego. Your ego makes you feel bad and behave badly, but your essential nature is goodness, just as God is goodness. In truth, your true self, the divine self, is the only self that exists, while the false self is a mirage.

You are not the false self. You are the divine self, but the divine self allows you to have the experience of being the false self. The divine self allows itself to become lost in the illusion of the false self until a certain point in your spiritual evolution when you awaken from this illusion. Most of humanity has yet to awaken, but many more people are awakening today than ever before.

What's difficult about loving yourself is loving the false self, the negative sense of self created by the ego and other conditioning. When you believe yourself to be this sense of self, you feel small, weak, lacking, unkind, judgmental, fearful, angry, and unhappy—and that self is difficult to love. What isn't difficult to love is your divine self—who you really are—because that self is pure goodness, pure love. Who you really are, your divine self, is completely lovable because your divine self *is* love.

Some people are easy to love because they reflect their divine nature so closely. The opposite is also true: The farther away people are from reflecting their divine nature (the more they reflect their egoic nature), the more difficult they are to love. You naturally love that which is of love, and you naturally shy away from or are repelled by that which is not of love.

Everyone has an ego, and the ego is not of love. The ego is also not evil, although it is behind all acts you would consider evil. The ego is not a thing or an entity; it's just programming to take care of #1. This programming causes you to be self-serving, self-centered, fearful, distrusting, defensive, and aggressive.

The ego is just a sense of self, however, not something real or true. A sense of self is nothing tangible, nothing that can't be fairly easily overlooked if its lack of realness is pointed out. The ego is programming that causes you to see life, yourself, and others through a particular lens, one tainted by fear, judgment, limitation, smallness, and a sense of lack.

The egoic programming creates a sense of being under attack or threatened by others and by life. The ego is in fear much of the time and, therefore, divorced from love. This fear is an illusion, an imagination of something fearful in the future, not based on an actual threat in the here and now.

However, when you are identified with this very primitive part of yourself, you believe in the ego's fears and try to protect yourself any way you can, usually by trying to attain more wealth, comfort, power, security, control, success, popularity, and admiration—all things that make the ego feel safer, at least temporarily.

Everyone knows what the ego is and what it feels like because the egoic state of consciousness is the state most people live in—but not always. Sometimes the ego relaxes—you relax—and you return home to your divine nature. You feel at peace, you are content and happy, you feel good—until the ego returns, and you feel lacking, afraid, striving, stressed-out, discontent, confused, and unhappy once again.

These are two very different states of consciousness, which everyone is aware of: the state of being identified with your ego and the state of being identified with your divine self. The spiritual path and spiritual growth are all about learning to shift your state and express your divine self increasingly in the world.

It is impossible to truly love yourself when you're identified with the ego. You can feel good about yourself and good in general momentarily—proud and elated over some success. But if loving yourself is dependent on winning or achieving something, then you'll never love yourself or feel good for long before you'll need to win or achieve something else to feel that way again. When you're identified with the ego, loving yourself is a fleeting experience.

Sadly, the love for yourself, or pride, that comes from winning often doesn't translate into being more loving or kind, into "loving your neighbor as yourself." Instead, many who've achieved something of merit hold themselves above and apart from others. No, feeling good about yourself for having achieved something is not the kind of love that leads to loving your neighbor.

Being proud of yourself is not the same as loving yourself. Feeling good about yourself is feeling good about the false self, and involvement with the false self can never lead to truly loving yourself or your neighbor. And unlike love, pride doesn't actually feel good, which is proof that pride comes from the ego.

The only thing capable of loving anything, including oneself, is the divine self, the Christ within you, the goodness/Godness within you. The ego doesn't know how to love, not even itself. To love yourself, you must be in touch with that which loves: the Divine within you.

That could be particularly difficult if you don't believe that the Divine—God—resides within you, that Christ abides in you as well as in me. If you believe that you are a sinner and separate from God, as many Christians are taught, you may not be aware of your own divinity, of your own inherent loving nature, as much as you could be. In truth, God is not separate from you. You are God as much as I am. You are an expression of God.

It's ironic that Christianity extols love but makes it difficult for people to love themselves by telling them they are sinners, by keeping them tied to fear, and by holding me up as the only son of God, when I was not. I was different from most only because I had realized the truth of my divine nature. The reason I came was to show you how to bring your Christ-like attributes forward and live as I did. I was and am a model for what you can be. I did not come to be worshipped.

Yes, you have an ego, but that is not your essential nature. Your essential nature is divine, and that's what is capable of the unconditional love that I am known for, although like every other human being, I was not perfect. The love that is within me is also within you. Love is your true nature as much as it is mine. That means that it is possible for you to love as I did.

This was my message, not that you are sinners and the only possibility for happiness is in heaven. No, I came to earth to show you that it's possible to love your neighbor as yourself and to encourage you to do so. I came to earth, not to bring love and then leave, but to ignite the love within you, to show you that you, too, could be Christed as I was and as I am. It is your destiny to live as love, and I came to show you how to do that. That was and is the purpose of my teachings.

To live as love, you must learn to go to that place within you that loves. You must learn to change your state, to disidentify with the ego. What allows you to drop into that place, that state, where love resides? Watching a beautiful sunset? Playing with your dog? Listening to an inspiring piece of music? Feeling the earth under your feet in the woods? Staring at a fire in the fireplace? Singing a song? Watching the clouds change shape? Looking at the night sky? Laughing with friends? Watching the snow fall? Reading a story to your child? Painting a picture? Playing an instrument? Dancing? Shooting baskets? You all know this state of love, peace, joy, and contentment and experience it often throughout your day. You all know and experience love, however briefly.

So many things are capable of bringing you to that place of love within you, very mundane things. But that's the point: Life—real life, mundane things—brings you into your loving heart. Whenever you are absorbed in life and lose yourself, your false self, in doing or just being, then love shows up. The only time that love is inaccessible is when you're lost in egoic thoughts, the voice in your head: thoughts about the past and future, thoughts of fear and limitation, and thoughts about *me, myself,* and *I*. Then, you *become* the false self.

Doing the simple things to return to love that I just listed, and many others, are not difficult, out-of-reach, or even costly. And yet, many go a long time without taking the time to do these things or do them for any length of time. These types of things should and can be part of everyone's daily life, but they often aren't. This accounts for much of the malaise in society. Society is sick as a result of a lack of contact with the Divine, a lack of feeling connected with love, peace, and joy.

This lack of connection with what is real, true, and meaningful, with your divine nature, is becoming even more of an issue because of the amount of time people, including children, are spending in front of computers and TVs. These engage and entertain the mind, but they don't feed the soul, and more often than not, they reinforce the ego's way of seeing and handling life.

There is, of course, a place for entertainment and information gathering, but it comes at quite a high cost to your spiritual life these days. People too easily become addicted to the intense mental stimulation that's so readily available today and then find the simple things that would bring them into their divine self uninteresting, which these simple things are to the mind.

If you feed your mind intensity, it will want more intensity, and then it seems like that's all you want. That may be all your mind wants, but it isn't all your *being* wants, all you need as a human being.

Extensive involvement in mental activities divorces you from real life, not only from relationships with real people, but from the very real experience of your divine self's joy, love, peace, and compassion—and from the guidance you need for how to live your life from a place of love. Humanity is experiencing a spiritual crisis, and technology, in many ways, is contributing to this and not likely to be what solves it.

Without touching into love regularly, you cannot be happy. You need love like you need the air you breathe, and almost as often. Many things can bring you happiness briefly—that brownie or that smile from your neighbor—but unless you consciously choose to make time each day for things that bring you into love, nothing else will satisfy you, and you'll continue to search for fulfillment in all the wrong places: entertainment, shopping, food, sex, alcohol, drugs, success, achievements, or just being busy.

These activities provide temporary relief from the ego's fears and negativity. They help you escape from the voice in your head's incessant chatter or help you feel good about your false self briefly. These things are not the answer, though, as you have probably discovered.

The answer lies in taking time daily to do some of the very simple things I just mentioned and the other many activities that are not ego-driven but inspired by your divine nature. Your true self loves the world and delights in the life it's been given.

It loves to play, create, laugh, grow, try new things, explore, learn, and also just rest and do nothing.

Like a child, the divine self relishes and revels in life. To the divine self, existence is wondrous, amazing, and a great gift, for which the divine self feels immense gratitude. And when you're aligned with your divine self, that is your experience of life as well.

The divine self is the source of joy, peace, love, compassion, patience, kindness, strength, courage, and every positive quality you can think of. And when you're aligned with it, you express these qualities. You become your best self. On the other hand, there is life as your ego experiences it and as you experience life when you're identified with your ego.

The world of the ego—the world of *me, myself,* and *I* and all the thoughts that create the story of *me*—is a world of illusion. It is a mental world, where you exist as someone who has problems, fears, fantasies, desires, and stories about yourself and others. This *me* and this world seem real, but they are an imaginary reality, not reality.

When you're engaged with the voice in your head, you experience an alternative reality, one full of negative thoughts and emotions. The voice in your head spins a reality in which you exist apart from love and connection with God. In that reality, you are alone and on your own in a scary world. You are imperfect and challenged and probably unhappy. You aren't experiencing real life as it's unfolding in the present moment, but your mind's story about "your" life.

Reality is much simpler and much more satisfying than the ego's mental world. Reality is whatever you're experiencing right now through your senses and intuitively, not what you're thinking or what your thoughts are causing you to experience or feel.

The problem is that your egoic mind makes life personal. It puts *you*, your false self, at the center of life, and life becomes all about what your ego likes and wants, as opposed to what *is*. That's what the voice in your head does. It makes the simple experience of this moment all about *you*. It turns life into a drama, just like in the movies, with *you* as the central character. This is how you become ensnared in the world of the ego and the false self.

Meanwhile, in addition to this drama, here you are, also existing as your true self and aware of and experiencing real life. The divine self is what is awake and aware of everything that's going on. It's alert, curious, and interested in everything. It's even interested in the egoic drama, but not exclusively, since it also loves to play in the real world of the senses and the here and now.

Love belongs to this real world, not to the world of the ego, because love is real. This may sound strange, since love is so intangible and difficult to define. Love isn't a thing with a color and shape. It's an *experience*, and that's what makes love real, as opposed to thoughts. Experiences are more real than thoughts, which take you into a virtual reality. Unlike anything else, thoughts have the capacity to take you into another reality, one that is *not* real.

Please understand that I'm not suggesting that your rational mind or creative imagination are anything but great gifts and useful tools. I'm talking about the voice in your head, which is distinct from these other aspects of mind. What I'm saying is that people tend to get lost in the world spun by the voice in their head. This takes them away from their real, present moment experience and away from the love, wisdom, courage, compassion, peace, and other qualities of their divine nature, which can't be accessed through thought.

The ego's world is not a rational world but a pre-rational and irrational world. The programming behind the ego is primitive programming that humanity is outgrowing. You don't need the voice in your head to define you or to tell you what to do or what to think or what to want, or to frighten you. The voice in your head isn't what keeps you safe but only pretends to be able to.

The voice in your head reflects humanity's basest instincts, not its highest expression. It's time for humanity to step into a higher state, one free of fear, compulsions, aggression, and negative emotions, a state similar to the one I abided in most of the time when I was on earth. It is possible now for many of you to advance significantly in your spiritual evolution because these difficult times demand this.

Humanity has reached a crossroads, and it will no longer be able to continue unless humanity's behavior changes quite dramatically, as human beings are destroying the very matrix that sustains them. Those of us guiding humanity are concerned about this and doing everything we can to ensure humanity's survival.

The power of nature to transform consciousness should not be underestimated. Contact with nature, such as sitting or walking in nature, is one of the surest ways to return to the love of your divine nature. You are part of nature, but buildings, roads, cars, TVs, and computers have divorced people from nature, and that isn't healthy. People are comfortable and safe, but they are disconnected from their Source and, therefore, from love. The ego has acquired so much of what it has wanted—safety, security, comfort, beauty, entertainment, pleasure—but at a cost.

Many people don't know who they are. They aren't in touch with their divine nature, not only because they have an ego, but also because society has elevated the ego's desires to such a degree that your lives revolve around these desires, leaving little time and energy for what is truly nourishing and enriching.

It wasn't always this way. People weren't always so ego-driven but lived closer to nature. This spiritual disease is an illness of more modern times, of industrial and technological advancement. The modern world was designed by the ego for the ego and reflects its values. Somehow, people need to return to basics. This doesn't necessarily mean giving up your comforts, but making room in your lives for what is real and for what really matters—in a word: love.

The way back to love is to reconnect with nature, but also to connect with the simple and real experience of this moment, whether you are in nature or not. Make time daily to contact the love that is within you in whatever ways work best for you. For some, it will be spending more time in nature or with loved ones or pets. For others, it might be just sitting and being, listening to or playing music, dancing, singing, writing poetry, or creating something else. For anyone who is serious about this, meditation is the most efficient way to learn to detach from the ego and experience your true nature.

Learn to find your way to this love and make time to experience it. When your actions and speech flow from this state of consciousness, you will be happy and truly fulfilled. Your life will be guided by wisdom, love, and compassion, and that will benefit you and everyone around you. When you are full of love, you become a magnet that attracts love and goodwill into your life. It all begins with loving yourself enough to turn away from the false self and connect with the love within you.

Without this connection to your divine nature, your life will not go as well, which means that other people's lives will not go as well either. Your state of consciousness affects everyone else's. When you are in right relationship with God, with love, then those around you can more easily be as well.

Loving yourself is not a selfish thing. The love of your divine nature is not about *you* at all, for the false self disappears in this kind of love. The false self dissolves, and all that remains is love. Loving yourself means loving the goodness—Godness— within you, and that's easy to do. It's even easy to love, or at least have compassion for, the false self when you aren't caught up in it.

When you are in touch with the love of your divine nature, love flows from you to everything. You feel connected to everything that your love is touching. You experience yourself as nowhere and everywhere, and you and what you are loving are felt to be one and the same. You experience a unity with life, with no separate *you* that is experiencing this. This is the ultimate experience, and you all have had it or can have it to one extent or another.

When you're connected to your divine self, who or what you are loving becomes irrelevant because the experience of loving is so fulfilling. When you are experiencing the love of your divine self, all boundaries disappear, and you naturally "love your neighbor," and that love will be pure and unconditional.

When you are aligned with your divine self, you are aligned with God and with the Whole. From there, you'll receive your "marching orders": what to do next, what to say, and how to be in the world. Who knows what the divine self will do once you allow it to be expressed through you?

"Love your neighbor as yourself" means love your neighbor as your divine self would. What would your divine self do? How would *it* behave toward your neighbor? How or what would it give or not give to someone? How would it speak? Many of you have asked, "What would Jesus do?" which is a similar question. When you allow it, your divine self acts spontaneously toward others in ways that benefit the Whole. Just as you have allowed your ego to be expressed through you, you can learn to allow your divine self to be expressed by you. Who knows what it will do? You don't know until your divine self acts.

There is a *you* that chooses who or what is in charge: the ego or the divine self. This *you* is very mysterious isn't it? This *you* is the divine self awakening within you. Describing these things is a bit tricky, since language wasn't designed to speak about the Mystery but only further shrouds it.

I lived according to the will of my divine self, the will of the Father, not the will of the ego, and you can as well. That is the only difference between you and me. I was no more God than you, but I had actualized the God force within.

Before you've gained some awareness, there seems to be little choice—the ego is in charge because you believe you *are* the false self. But once the divine self has been actualized or activated to some extent, it can begin to operate more freely in your life.

This actualization—this shift from ego to the divine self—is a process that takes time, effort, and conscious choice. It doesn't happen overnight. Spiritual development requires continual vigilance toward the voice in your head. You have to become aware of what it's asking you to believe and choose to not believe that. The ability to be aware and to choose in this way develops by exercising your awareness and choice, just as a muscle is developed by using it. There is no other way. To awaken from the ego, each of you must do this work.

Once you are committed to this process and spiritual forces see this, they come forward to support you. As you develop the connection to your divine self, you draw to you more and more help from those in higher dimensions whose purpose it is to support this process in human beings. These are not your usual guides but others who specialize in this stage of spiritual development. Be sure to call on them for help whenever you need it.

It's a momentous time in one's spiritual evolution when one begins to awaken to the Truth and throw off the shackles of the ego. Every soul eventually reaches this important turning point. Many of you are at this point and ready to become who you are meant to be, to become the Christed human being you can be.

I need to add that a Christed, or enlightened, human being today doesn't necessarily look like what you suppose I looked like when I was alive. Yes, I did perform some miracles, mostly for healing and to demonstrate what's possible when you are connected to God, or enlightened. This doesn't mean you will also be able to perform similar miracles when you awaken from your ego or become enlightened.

I was crucified in large part for stirring up an impassioned following, one that threatened the status quo. The miracles contributed greatly to the passion the masses felt toward me and, consequently, to my early demise. I knew this would happen, for I knew my destiny beforehand.

The awakened or enlightened human being today will not necessarily display such extraordinary gifts, for it would be disruptive to his or her purpose and, therefore, counterproductive. The awakened or enlightened human being today will appear quite ordinary and may not attract much attention or have great mass appeal, given the materialistic nature of your world. He or she will be flawed and imperfect, just as I was, although little was written about how human I was, since that would have undermined the Church's narrative that I was the one and only son of God.

It is a myth that I was more holy and perfect than a human being could possibly be. I was a human being, and those who awaken and become enlightened, as I did, are still human beings, who will always have an ego and the potential to become identified with it. Awakened and enlightened human beings can still feel angry and deeply sad at times, but they don't feel those feelings for long or act on them in harmful ways; that's the difference. Enlightened human beings still have the capacity to feel emotions, but their emotions don't rule them.

Many are awakening today. There may be people close to you who are already awake or awakening, and you may not be aware of it. As a result of awakening and enlightenment, people become more loving and at peace, more easy-going, and freer, but that may not be particularly remarkable to those around them. This shift in consciousness, although obvious to the one it has happened to, isn't always obvious to others because that shift is internal.

Spiritual awakening is a shift in one's relationship to the ego and, therefore, in one's perceptions of life. This shift in the lens through which one views life will also certainly affect someone's behavior, but as I said, he or she won't necessarily walk on water or heal the sick or give inspiring speeches to the masses.

If you knew yourself as love, which is the truth, would you have difficulty loving yourself? It's only because you believe the voice in your head's definition of yourself and follow its bad advice that you don't love yourself. This voice is continually telling you that you are lacking, not good enough, in danger, and needing life and others to be other than the way they are before you can be happy.

This is why you aren't happy and don't love yourself. That's all—just this voice, which is similar in everyone's head. This voice makes everyone feel discontent, unhappy, and bad about themselves. And it wreaks havoc in relationships. If you listen to this voice and believe it, it will be difficult for you to love yourself and others. This is the nature of the human disease. It starts with the voice in your head, the ego's voice, and all suffering follows from there.

Unlike the ego's selfishness and negativity, the divine self has qualities that are easy to love—in you and in everyone else: goodness, kindness, love, compassion, acceptance, curiosity, a willingness to grow, courage, joy, playfulness, and creativity. These qualities are what is lovable in you and in others and what makes loving yourself and others possible. When you focus on these qualities, love flows to yourself and others.

Here are two practices that will help you shift from the ego to love:

- ❖ Spend some time quietly repeating this or something like this: *"I am love, love, love. The love of God surrounds me and permeates me. I am this love that is God. There is nothing but this love within and without, and nothing can harm this love. I am an embodiment of love. I live for love and express love in all I say and do."*

- ❖ Here's a practice that will be very useful and powerful for you, which you can do in meditation, as you lie awake in bed, or even while driving or doing other things during your day:

Energy is the substratum of life, and this energy is love. It could also be said to be light. "Love" and "light" are words for the same thing, but these words evoke different experiences within you. "Light" helps you *see* or visualize this energy, and "love" helps you feel the true nature of this energy. So, I will use both of these words now in this practice because I want you to both see and feel the nature of this energy.

The practice is a simple one, and it includes your breath, which will help you stay anchored in your body and in the present moment. So now, as you breathe in slowly and deeply, without straining or trying to control your breath, but breathing in a very relaxed and natural way, imagine that love and light are flowing into your crown chakra, the top of your head, as you say (mentally to yourself), "I am love and light." Breathe in love and light as you slowly inhale and say those words and imagine that love and light are infusing and recharging every cell of your body. And then, as you exhale slowly, once again say, "I am love and light" again and imagine that love and light are overflowing and pouring out from every cell of your body into the world.

As you do this, your body and subtle body literally fill with the love and light of the Creator, until it overflows to the world. This love and light is healing in every way. It is rejuvenating and will bring you refreshment and connect you with the Source, the Oneness, God, with All That Is and help you be a beacon of love in the world—for what good would it do if you have love and light and others do not? Love and light will naturally fill you and spill from you to others, simply because you have called upon it to do so. You cannot receive in this way without it affecting the rest of creation.

If, at first, you don't feel the love and light moving through you, no problem. Some people feel this right away, while for others, this takes some time to develop. The more you practice this, the better you'll get at experiencing this flow. Practicing this will develop this circuit so that eventually the flow will be experienced instantly, as soon as you state, "I am love and light." But first, most of you will have to practice this a while to build this circuit within you. Spending time doing this acknowledges your intention to be love and light in the world. And the more you do this, the more you'll be used in this way.

The reason this practice works is that the love and light of creation is real. When you imagine it moving through you in this way, it does. It moves this way because you have intended it to move this way. You have evoked it. You have commanded it. Usually you use your mind to imagine things the ego wants or fears. However, the *you* that is awakening can choose to use your imagination this way instead, to invoke and invite the creative force of love to flow through you. This is a powerful act.

It is your destiny to learn to bring in love and light this way. Everyone, in one lifetime or another, eventually learns the secret of this simple technique or something similar. People generally learn this from spiritual teachers or masters, those who understand the workings of the universe. You must reach a point in your evolution where you are open to this knowledge. When you begin to cooperate with the forces that are assisting your evolution in this way by doing such a practice, your evolution can speed up exponentially. Love and light are a gift to you and everyone, but you have to invite love and light to enter your life in this way.

So, don't let the simplicity of this practice fool you. It will empower you to become the love-bearer and light-bearer that you are destined to be. Many of you have come to earth specifically to be that in your own way. And others can benefit from this practice by healing themselves and becoming more of who they are meant to be.

You are amazing and beautiful beings, each and every one of you, and I am merely helping you to realize this, to realize your true nature, which is no different than mine. We are the same. We are love. Let us get on with being this love in the world now. Practicing what I have just taught you will advance you quickly to this end.

Chapter 2

Loving Your Neighbor

The reason for these teachings is that human beings have difficulty loving each other. That is obvious. But why? Why is it so difficult to love? It's not that you are unloving or even that you need to learn to love, but that you have an ego that is unloving, vindictive, petty, judgmental, selfish, and unkind. Your ego is that way, not you.

The negativity that causes all of humanity's suffering is programmed into humanity, and it's called the ego. I won't go into why this is so at this time except to say that this programming provides the challenge that forces people to find another way to behave. That way is love. The ego gives you the experience of what being divorced from love is like, and as one song so wisely says, "You don't know what you've got till it's gone."

Your soul has chosen the challenge of having an ego for any number of reasons. It's best to assume that you have freely chosen to be a human being on earth to grow in ways you need to grow and in ways your soul has gladly taken on. To take the ego's perspective, which would be to feel victimized by your ego, is only to create more suffering. The ego plays both the persecutor and the victim.

If there were not another way of seeing life and being in life than the ego's way, this situation would be—and is, for some—a living hell. But that is not the case. There is a way out of the suffering caused by the ego, and that is love.

Love is the way to everything you have ever wanted, but the ego doesn't see that. Loving makes the ego feel even more vulnerable than it already feels. It makes the ego feel weak and, therefore, unsafe. The only way the ego will allow itself to love another is if it seems that will result in more of what the ego wants: security, safety, status, recognition, material comfort, pleasure, beauty, power—and yes, love.

The ego does want love, but it wants love on its own terms. In other words, the ego is willing to be loved, but it isn't willing to give up control or any of the other things it prizes in exchange for love. The ego won't choose love over power, money, status, safety, or comforts. So, if it sees love or a relationship as a threat to these or not capable of providing these, then it will bow out, withhold love, or not get involved.

It's easy to love those who don't threaten you but support and love you, and so the ego is willing to engage in those types of relationships until it no longer gets its way. Fortunately, the true self, which chooses love over all else, exists within everyone unceasingly and is experienced alongside the ego. When you love someone and your ego is challenged, you experience both the love your true self has for that person and your ego's anger or upset and withdrawal of love.

This is what makes love so confusing: You both love and don't love someone at the same time. This is because you are dual creatures, you could say. You are both human and divine. You are divine *and* you have an ego. You love *and* you judge and hate. This is the dilemma, the conflict you feel within yourself in relationships. It's good to be aware of this.

When you're by yourself, you're likely to struggle with a disparaging voice in your head. But when you're with others, this voice is more likely to disparage others as a way of feeling better about yourself and gaining the upper hand. For the ego, relationships are an opportunity to assert its power and feel superior, which is the ego's solution to not feeling good about itself—feelings that the ego caused itself to feel. Such is the tangled web the ego weaves!

It's no wonder that relationships are challenging, when the ego sees them as a means for attaining two very contradictory goals: superiority and love. The ego wants love *and* it wants control, power, and superiority—and that's a tall order! To make matters worse, the ego resents needing love from anyone and is unwilling to give any more than it has to.

It's a good thing that human beings aren't just their egos, or humanity would have never survived! Something else besides the ego is present in every interaction between two people, and that is the love of their divine nature. This love has sustained humanity throughout all the difficulties created by the ego and continues to draw people together in mutual cooperation.

The egoic programming is not stronger than your true nature, but this programming is a real problem in relationships, including between nations. Relationships bring out the ego like nothing else because they make it feel threatened. The ego is the cause of every conflict and behind every war.

There has never been a "holy" war, although sometimes people have had to fight to stop an unholy one. And so, at this stage in humanity's evolution, it has sometimes been necessary to fight against those who are determined to take power and freedom away from others.

Sometimes the ego has to be stopped by those who see it for what it is. However, being convinced that you're on the side of what's right and righteous is not evidence that you are, since that is also what the ego assumes. People are easily fooled by their egos. Most human beings are not developed enough to tell when their ego is in charge, and many assume it isn't when it is, if they even understand that much.

If the ego's tactics worked, that would be one thing, but the ego's tactics are counterproductive and often backfire. Let me give you an example. Let's say, you want your partner to be neater. The way your ego would handle this is to complain, criticize him or her, or seethe in anger and withhold affection. The problem with these tactics is that they either don't deliver the message clearly or they do it in a way that makes your partner's ego determined to criticize you, judge you, or argue with you. And nothing changes.

What happened to asking nicely? That would be the loving and rational thing to do, and much more effective. When you are rational and kind, your partner is much more likely to respond similarly and cooperate with you. In relationship, you get back what you put out: Criticism reaps criticism; kindness reaps kindness.

This is so obvious, and yet, your first response to your partner doing something you don't like will usually be the ego's response. That's good to know. Once you know that, you have more choice around that. Once you're more aware of the ego, it can't get away with as much, if you don't let it. That doesn't mean it's easy to override the programming. It isn't, and sometimes you won't succeed, and then you'll feel bad and so will your partner.

That's where apologies come in. Saying "I'm sorry" goes a long way in relationships. Forgiving yourself and your partner are key acts of emotional hygiene and necessary to maintaining relationships. Without forgiveness, a relationship will die slowly, if not quickly, because the ego will have gained the upper hand. With the ego in control, there is no gentleness, only pain and criticism, and love can't survive for long in such an atmosphere.

To maintain a relationship, you have to let go of the past, which the ego is unwilling to do. The ego hangs on to grievances because this is one of its ways of gaining the upper hand. "You did this to me" makes the ego feel righteous and superior. The ego loves to blame others and play the victim. Using such a strategy to gain power in a relationship doesn't make much sense, but the ego isn't rational, which is why its strategies often backfire.

The ego maintains power and, presumably, control in relationships by pointing out the partner's flaws and mistakes. To the ego, forgiving or letting go of someone's mistakes would be a missed opportunity to be right, righteous, and superior. The ego wants this feeling of righteousness and superiority more than it wants love, and since you can't have both, love loses out.

This bears repeating: You don't get to feel right and superior *and* have love, because these are mutually exclusive states of consciousness. Which one do you prefer? You have a choice, although it may not seem that way, because indulging the ego is so tempting. The ego tempts you to go against love with the slightly good feeling of being right and superior, or being mean.

The ego gets some pleasure from being mean or unkind, and this must be acknowledged. Are you willing to exchange love for this egoic pleasure? If, in the moment when you're tempted to be unkind, you recognized the cost of that fleeting pleasure to your relationship, you probably wouldn't choose to indulge in the ego's judgment, criticism, or anger.

Losing love is never worth the price you pay, but that's something everyone has to learn for themselves. You're told to be kind to others, but how many realize how very important kindness is? The thing is, being unkind can feel strong. You feel like you're standing up for something, but what you're standing up for is your ego. Being unkind is a power grab. The ego uses unkindness and anger to intimidate and manipulate others in an attempt to get its way.

To the ego, kindness and forgiveness feel like weakness, and the ego isn't capable of either. Only the divine self is capable of these. To forgive, you have to be in the present moment, something the ego avoids like the plague. When you are present, you're just here, now, experiencing life as it is and as your divine self is experiencing it, with no desires, no fears, no worries, no stories, no fantasies, and no past or future—in other words, no ego!

When you are in the now, there isn't anything to forgive, because you aren't carrying around a story of having been hurt or betrayed. By definition, being present is a lack of involvement in ideas about the past. If you aren't bringing the past into the present moment by thinking about it, the past can't cause you pain. You hurt *yourself* by dwelling on events that hurt you in the past.

It's the ego that tells stories about the past and dwells on them. The ego spins those stories in a particular way that feels painful. It could spin them differently, but it doesn't. In fact, spinning them differently, or reframing them, is one of the ways painful memories are rendered less painful.

Reframing heals pain from the past because it includes more than what the ego's story included. It includes a higher perspective, a more positive one, the perspective of your soul. This more inclusive perspective makes it easier to let go of an experience and be at peace. This author has written about reframing in more detail in *From Stress to Stillness* and several other books.

In telling painful stories, the ego's goal is to keep you in a negative emotional state. "Diabolical!" you say? Yes, the ego is that way, and it's best not to soft-pedal this. Seeing the truth about the ego disempowers it and empowers you to make other choices.

People suffer because they believe the painful version of history that their ego, through the voice in their head, tells them. Even if an event in the past was truly tragic, the ego creates unnecessary additional pain by repeatedly bringing up those memories. If you dwell on those painful memories and stories, they'll keep coming up, and you'll continue to suffer over them. Dwelling on them only reinforces them; it doesn't heal them. However, if you don't dwell on them, they'll eventually stop arising. This is how the egoic mind is healed—by not giving your attention to painful memories and stories. This isn't the same as repressing feelings. You are simply not feeding or regenerating feelings.

To forgive those who have harmed you and to heal, two things are necessary: Letting go of your thoughts about them and understanding that everyone who has ever harmed anyone was identified with the ego and its fear and ignorance. When I said, "Forgive them, for they know not what they do," I was referring to those who aren't aware of how their ego manipulates them through the voice in their head. They hurt others and themselves because they don't realize they have a choice around their thoughts and behavior. Instead, they take the path of least resistance.

Because your egoic programming is your default, the ego's way of behaving is automatic and feels natural, but it doesn't represent your best self or the best course of action. Most people are sleepwalking through life, not really consciously making decisions but acting on the impulse of their ego, which leads to very poor results.

Those who are operating so unconsciously suffer greatly and cause others to suffer along with them. If you become a victim of their suffering and bad behavior, forgiving them is the only way to unhook yourself from what they are creating. Otherwise, you end up like them, a victim of your own ego. The reason for forgiving others is to free yourself from the state of consciousness that caused the suffering in the first place.

Practically speaking, forgiveness is a matter of letting go of any thoughts about the past so that you can be in the here and now, free of suffering, and carry on in love. Forgiveness is not a one-time statement you make to someone, although that can be helpful, but a commitment to not indulging in the painful thoughts that perpetuate negative emotions (i.e. the egoic state) within you. To forgive, you must "forget" those thoughts—leave them be when they arise. Don't get involved with them. Living in the now, as your divine self does, means letting go of such thoughts and staying with your present moment experience.

The divine self (and you, when you are aligned with your divine self) feels only compassion for those who suffer at the hands of their own egos and who cause others to suffer. The divine self understands that, at this point in their evolution, it can be no other way. They're doing the best they can, and they will learn from their choices. What good would it do to take any other stance?

You can only hope that others will forgive you your errors and missteps as well: "Do unto others as you would have them do unto you." It's hard to be a human being, as I have so often said, and the situation deserves your compassion. Choosing to be compassionate toward those who have hurt or are hurting you and then returning to your present moment experience will allow you to feel the peace and love of your divine nature.

Eventually, people do learn from the suffering they cause themselves and others, but that can take a long time. How much better it would be if they understood how they're being manipulated by their own egos and how damaging this is to their relationships. With this understanding, people could evolve much more quickly than through trial and error. There's no need to suffer so much now, since this understanding is available. It's time to become free of the ego.

In relationships, the ego shows up as soon as differences or disagreements do, which is what makes loving your neighbor so challenging. The ego has little tolerance for differences unless they benefit it. To the ego, differences or disagreements are a reason for attacking, judging, diminishing, scapegoating, or making fun of others. The ego truly believes that if someone is different from it, he or she is bad or wrong.

This assumption of superiority is at the core of most problems in relationships. And when that's the case, the other person often feels the same sense of superiority. Then, the disagreement becomes about who is right and superior, not about the actual differences that need to be addressed or negotiated.

This superiority tends to get voiced as a judgment. Someone looks different or believes differently or does things differently than you would like, and you assume something bad about him or her. You tell a negative story about that person, one that is made up by the ego, which is essentially what a judgment is. Judgment is a weapon that is wielded to try to settle differences by claiming the moral high ground.

The way this high ground is claimed is through storytelling. I'm not talking about nice bedtime storytelling, but unkind and untrue storytelling. These stories are often disguised as insight, but they are lies because they're based on assumptions. Although there may be some evidence to back up these assumptions, the evidence is often very thin, based on a few experiences, and cherry-picked to build a case against someone. This phenomenon is very familiar to everyone.

Look at your judgments. Study them. This is how they work. They are largely assumptions that serve your ego in some way, usually by making you seem smart, insightful, right, or superior in some other way. There is no love in your judgments, even when you pretend to be judging someone out of concern or a supposed desire to help that person.

The ego is very tricky. Do not be deceived. Nearly every thought you have about others is a judgment or likely to turn into one if you think about someone long enough. This is also true in speaking about others when they aren't present, otherwise known as gossiping. Your thoughts and conversations about others may seem purposeful and well-intentioned, but more often than not, they are in service to the ego.

The ego knows how to hook you into doing its bidding—into judging—and one way it does this is by getting you to think about others and talk about others. The ego's goal is to sabotage your relationships, except occasionally when the goal is to wheedle its way in with someone who can be of benefit to it.

The ego is the worst type of narcissist. It does what it does because it expects some kind of benefit for it. It doesn't do things for love, since love is not one of the things the ego is most after. The ego will take love if love is offered, but love is not the ego's goal as much as other things.

The good news is that most human beings are not this taken over by their egos; they are not narcissists. Their divine self shines through some, if not much, of the time. Hooray for love! It is actually a powerful force in relationships, more powerful than the ego, or there would be no relationships whatsoever. But it's good to know what you're up against.

Some will chastise me for talking this way about the ego and say I should be kinder toward it. I'm not suggesting that you go to battle with the ego, for that would be the ego going to battle with itself. I'm suggesting that you be aware of the ego and what it's up to so that you aren't fooled by it and can make better choices about how to behave. Knowledge is power, and I seek to empower you. The ego is not that powerful. It is only ignorance of the ego that gives it power.

By all means, accept that you have an ego and that the ego is the way it is. However, you don't need to have compassion for the ego, because it isn't an entity; it's programming. What good is it to have compassion for programming? Have compassion for yourself and others for having an ego, but not for the ego itself. You don't have to love the ego, it doesn't need healing, and it won't be healed by your love and acceptance.

The benefit of accepting the ego is that acceptance aligns you with your divine self. Acceptance heals *you*, while going to battle with the ego will do nothing but keep you involved with it.

"Love your neighbor as yourself" means move beyond any differences between you and your neighbor and love him or her as you would love someone who was just like you, someone with whom you have no differences—which would be no one, since you are the only one in the world that you have no differences with!

Everyone else in the world throughout time has been different from you. This is why peace in relationships and in the world is so very difficult. The only solution is to accept and appreciate these differences rather than make them a reason to put someone out of your heart.

If you take the ego's stance, that those who are different from you are bad, a threat, or inferior, you'll be at war with everyone, and some people seem to be for that very reason. Those who are very ego-involved have great difficulty loving, and that's why. To the ego, differences are cause for judgment, and judgments close the heart to love. As a result, the ego's world is very lonely. The more involved you are in the ego's perceptions and beliefs, the less love you experience within yourself and coming to you from others.

You can only go so far in this direction before something has to give. The suffering of the egoic state of consciousness can be so great that some take their own lives, but that is no solution. The lesson of love still needs to be learned, and that soul will reincarnate and try again to make better choices.

There is no punishment awaiting someone who chooses suicide, although suicide is a lost opportunity for the soul and, therefore, discouraged. That person will receive healing, compassion, and instruction from guides on the other side. Usually, for those who have lost their way, what is needed for them to heal is love. So, in the next lifetime, that person may be placed in a particularly loving family or encounter people or experiences that make the truth about love evident.

Punishment is never part of one's lesson plan. Punishment is something humans engage in, in an attempt to reform someone. But the nonphysical beings who serve God by facilitating human evolution do not engage in punishment. It is a poor means of reform. It is cruel, and God is not cruel. God is synonymous with love.

To return to the subject of differences, the truth is that differences make life interesting, they are grist for your spiritual evolution, and they provide the soul with a variety of experiences. Not only that, but a society needs diversity to survive and thrive. A society needs all kinds of people with an array of interests and talents. Differences are good!

Differences seem problematic because they are problematic to the ego, but they don't have to be if you're able to view them from the divine self's perspective. Differences make the world go around. They're part of life. They make people unique. At best, differences are adorable, and at worst, they must be accepted.

From a higher perspective, all differences are superficial and not worth losing love over. Such differences are part of the costume each soul is wearing. What is the same about everyone is of much greater significance: the God force within each of you. That God force, the divine self, is what is lovable about everyone.

"Love your neighbor as yourself" means love your neighbor's true self. What is lovable about yourself and lovable about your neighbor is one and the same because your essence is one and the same. The great mystery at the core of life is that everything and everyone is an expression of the One, of God. God is manifesting through all life. The same God force is in everything, and that God force is supremely loveable. See yourself—your true self—in your neighbor and love that. Recognize that your neighbor is essentially the same as you.

When two people are truly in love, that God force, or essential goodness, is exactly what they are in love with. They may love specific things about each other, but the deep and lasting love they feel for each other, which binds them together through any difficulties and differences, is based on the experience of the other as one's own self. When you are with someone for a long time, the boundaries fade, and he or she begins to feel like your very own self, like a part of you. Those who lose someone they have been with a very long time know what this feels like.

That is love. Then, treating the other with respect and as you would like to be treated comes naturally, although the ego can still rise up at any time. When you experience another as yourself, being with that person is as comfortable as being with yourself, because you can relax. Why is that so? Because the other person accepts you and allows you to be as you are. That acceptance is the essence of love. This brings us to our next chapter and our next exploration: "Do unto others as you would have them do unto you."

Chapter 3

The Golden Rule

"Do unto others as you would have them do unto you" is known as the Golden Rule. This is something I taught long ago and many others have taught over the ages. The Golden Rule is a way of measuring your behavior. You can ask, "Does doing this follow the Golden Rule?"

People need a measure for their behavior because the ego is very tricky. For instance, judging often feels smart, just, discriminating, and possibly helpful, when it isn't. "Judge not lest you be judged" is not just a warning that whomever you judge will judge you back, but a guide for behavior in keeping with the Golden Rule. You don't want to be judged, so don't judge others. Judging is neither helpful nor loving.

The Golden Rule works because it's easy to know what you would want "done unto you" or not "done unto you." Every human being is pretty much the same as far as that goes. Some experiences are universally desirable, while others are not.

However, it's a little more complicated than that. For instance, someone might give you a gift, thinking it would make you happy because it would make that person happy, when that wasn't something you wanted. Or someone might do something to you that you felt was rude, but that person didn't intend it that way. Minor differences between people make the Golden Rule somewhat imperfect, but it may be the best guideline you have.

The Golden Rule can be understood to mean two things: Do to others what you would like others to do to you, and don't do to others what you don't want done to you. The Golden Rule suggests acting positively toward others: Be loving, forgiving, kind, generous, gentle, helpful, compassionate, respectful, patient, attentive, and so forth. And it suggests not acting negatively toward others: Don't kill, hurt, lie, or steal, and don't be unkind, judgmental, hateful, unforgiving, threatening, impatient, disrespectful, and so forth.

I have emphasized and do emphasize the first way of understanding the Golden Rule because behaving positively toward others cultivates love, and love will fulfill you and make the world a happier place. Refraining from negative acts will also improve the world, but it won't do much for your soul's evolution or in making this a happier or more enlightened world. People who restrain their egos do less damage in the world than those you don't, but if restraining their egos is all they do, they'll remain in the egoic state of consciousness, and so will humanity. They won't be free.

I came to teach a better way to live than just restraining the ego. I came to bring you the truth that will set you free, and that truth is love. To move out of the egoic state of consciousness and into a state of divine grace and love requires more than not doing something—restraining the ego. It requires making some conscious choices to do certain things.

First, you have to choose to examine your thoughts. You need to recognize that whatever you are believing, whether it's a judgment, a story, or a negative thought, is a lie. It's the ego's spin on life, and it doesn't serve. Then, once you are aware that you're caught up in such a thought, you have to choose to turn away from it, say no to it. This involves giving your attention to something else instead—not to another thought, but to something more real than thoughts: to love.

As intangible as love is, it is very real and always available whenever you turn your attention to it. However, you can't get to love by thinking about it. In fact, thinking about love or about anything takes you away from love. This is because love doesn't reside in the realm of your mind and imagination but in a very different realm, which I and others call the subtle realm.

The subtle realm is the realm of the spiritual Heart and where your divine self lives. I say "realm," which sounds esoteric, but this realm is no different from your present moment experience. If you drop out of the mental realm and are no longer lost in thoughts, you land in the sensory realm, the world of the body and senses. The sensory world is the gateway to the subtle realm of energy and extrasensory experience. The subtle realm includes such things as intuitions, inspiration, energetic experiences, creative urges and other deep drives, and all the qualities of the divine self. This sensory and extrasensory experience is also known as real life!

The experience of real life is often overlooked because thoughts are experienced as "louder" than the experience of real life and felt to be more interesting. Just as TV and movies are more interesting and compelling to the mind than real life, thoughts are more interesting and compelling to your mind than your real-life sensory and extrasensory experience.

People leave real life and go into thought because the default is to listen to the voice in your head. This means that most people live in a virtual reality most of the time rather than reality. The problem with this is that love, peace, wisdom, and every other quality of your divine self are not accessed through thought but only through real life. These gifts from your divine self exist only in the subtle realm.

The mental realm is made up of thoughts. It's an alternate reality, one largely designed by and reflective of the ego and other conditioning. And yet, because the mental world is your default, this world seems real to you. The ego's desires, stories, fears, and beliefs all feel very real and true, while there is nothing real and true about the ego's world.

Love is found in reality, and reality is an *experience,* not a thought or imagination. Love is an experience, and if love is an experience you want (the ego doesn't), then you must go to love, for love won't come seeking you if you choose to reside in the mental realm. You have to choose to experience love. Many spend their lives longing for and dreaming about love, while ironically, those very thoughts prevent them from experiencing love.

How do you choose love? Simply turn your attention away from thoughts to the realm in which love resides. This is a matter of experiencing whatever your body is experiencing on a sensory, energetic, and intuitive level. Notice what you are experiencing and then look for the experience of love. It's there, within you, as a subtle energetic experience. Love might feel like joy or an expansion in your heart or a warm, relaxing feeling. You know what love feels like.

Right now, can you find love, however slight that experience might be? When you do, focus on that subtle experience in your body, and it will become more prominent. Whatever you give your attention to is magnified. Then, stay in touch with love by keeping your attention on that subtle experience. This is a particularly good practice to do when you are with others, when the tendency to go into judgment and other thoughts is so tempting.

This practice isn't hard to do, but you have to choose to do it. This practice can become automatic and very natural, but it usually needs to be done consistently for a while before that happens. The biggest challenge is not getting hijacked by the voice in your head. If that happens, just return to sensing the subtle experience of love within you.

Overcoming the default is accomplished by doing the opposite of the default. The default compels you to think about yourself and your life, judge, evaluate, compare, worry, desire, and go into the past and future. What's the opposite of that? Not having such thoughts isn't an option, since you're not in control of what thoughts arise and when. What you *are* in control of is whether you stay involved with those thoughts. Since the default is giving your attention to thoughts, the opposite of that is giving your attention to *anything but* your thoughts. Doing that will help undo or neutralize the default. The "anything but" is real life.

Imagine all the times you've gotten lost in thoughts. A lot, right? So, it's understandable that it would take a lot of practice to neutralize the default. Unfortunately, there's no other way to freedom, love, and your inner wisdom than the practice of turning your attention away from thoughts to the present moment.

Let's talk about inner wisdom. Moment to moment, you are being guided by higher spiritual forces. Although I, Jesus, don't act as a personal guide for people as much as a world teacher and healer, many, many other higher dimensional beings are charged with providing individual guidance. Where they are guiding people is toward love. Essentially, the journey you are on is a return to love, a return to your inherent divinity.

These higher dimensional beings guide people primarily through their intuition, which some refer to as the Holy Spirit. Everyone is aware of the nudges, urges, inspiration, excitement, joy, and "ah-has" that are used to guide you each day, even if not everyone heeds them. This means of guidance is no secret. Science may not be able to measure it, and schools may not teach it, but everyone is aware that something is going on that could be construed as guidance. And so, it is. This is the truth. The deepest mysteries of life cannot be quantified or adequately described in words, which is why the truth is often overlooked or dismissed.

You are being lovingly guided, and this guidance is trustworthy. What isn't trustworthy is the advice the voice in your head offers. It's a little like those 8-balls some of you had as children, where you shake them and an answer pops up. The voice in your head isn't much more trustworthy than that.

The voice in your head is essentially programming, and what does programming know about living life, especially about living it in a way that fulfills you and your soul's plan? What does programming know about love? The voice in your head doesn't even know how to make you happy.

To return to the Golden Rule, it is best applied to how you are with others: Be with and treat others in the way that you would like others to be with and treat you. The Golden Rule is less useful as a guideline for how to help others and give to them, which I'll say more about in a bit.

You know how you would like others to be with you and treat you. You would like them to be kind, patient, attentive, accepting, compassionate, forgiving, and respectful, and you don't want them to be the opposite. That's a pretty good and simple formula for how to be in relationship with others. These are all attributes of love, aren't they? If someone is kind, patient, attentive, accepting, compassionate, forgiving, and respectful, they are behaving lovingly toward you, and you will probably feel loved by them and feel love *for* them.

Knowing that this is the formula for love, is it so difficult to be this way in relationship? It's difficult for the ego but natural for the divine self. What stands in the way is that your programming causes you to focus on getting something from others when you're with them, not on fostering love. You may think that love is what you care about, but love isn't what your ego cares about, and it's useful to observe that in your interactions with others.

When you are with others, how interested are you in getting attention and speaking about yourself versus being attentive and interested in others? Love listens. Love is open, attentive, interested, and curious about others. Love shares information that might be helpful, but not for self-glorification or any other selfish reason.

When you are with others, two very different ways of being with them are possible, depending on what you are giving your attention to within yourself: your thoughts about yourself or your present moment experience. As I said, people are dual creatures: They are both egoically motivated and divinely motivated. Both kinds of motivations or drives exist simultaneously within you in any moment, but because the ego is the default, the ego's motives usually predominate or are at least felt first.

It's good to realize that there's more to you than your ego, and more to others than theirs. In every interaction, something else is present besides the ego, and that is the divine self. Once you are more aware of this duality within you, you have more choice about how you are with others. Will you behave as your ego, your false self, or will you behave as your divine self?

Staying connected to your divine self in the presence of others is complicated by the fact that most people are identified with their egos, and that can easily draw out yours. When people encounter each other, the ego is usually the first on the scene.

This tendency to identify with your ego when you are around others is overcome by simply noticing this. Notice that your ego is right there with its criticisms, comparisons, evaluations, and judgments. That's your ego doing that, not your divine intelligence, and it's not doing this out of love, but sizing the other up to see how you measure up.

Just notice this, and then find that which is within you that is curious about this encounter: "What will happen next? What will this person say or do? What will I say or do?" The divine self is a curious witness to life. It doesn't pretend to have answers to these questions but eagerly awaits what it will discover.

When the divine self has something to say, it jumps into conversations with wisdom, lightness, love, playfulness, gentleness, acceptance, and compassion. Your divine self and someone else's can be recognized by those qualities. The divine self often brings a higher or more light-hearted perspective than the usual one, and what is spoken rings true and makes everyone relax and feel at ease.

The divine self is a channel for wisdom and love in the world, and if you align with it, you will be used as such a channel. This is very different than you being used by the ego, which spreads hate, fear, anger, judgment, prejudices, and other negativity. There, in the last two sentences, is that mysterious *you* again. *You* are either an instrument of the ego or of the divine self. And *you* can choose.

Before you are awakened, you are an instrument and expression of the ego more than the divine self, but not exclusively. After spiritual awakening, you become an instrument and expression of the divine self, and only occasionally express the ego in detrimental ways. That is the difference before and after spiritual awakening.

I hasten to add that it's not your fault that you are used by the ego. It can be no other way. You are designed with the ego as your default, and until you are ready to awaken, you will go through the lessons and trials associated with this. So, please be compassionate with yourself and others. "Forgive them for they know not what they do" and forgive yourself. The challenge of having an ego creates the drama, difficulties, and experiences your soul needs and is willing to have in order to grow in certain ways. There is no mistake in this. This is part of everyone's divine plan.

How to be in relationship is clear from the Golden Rule: Be with and treat others in a way that you would like them to be with you and treat you. However, as for how to help and give to others in specific circumstances, the Golden Rule isn't as helpful. It isn't always the case that doing something for someone that you would want done for you would be beneficial or what someone wants or in someone's best interests.

For instance, giving someone something you would like isn't necessarily what that person would like or need. Or giving your child cookies when she's sad isn't really in her best interest. Even giving someone help when asked might not be what that soul needs to grow. Indiscriminate giving can cause dependency and stunt someone's growth.

Fortunately, you've been provided with a moment-to-moment guidance system that helps you determine what to do, what to give, and what to say in specific circumstances. The catch is that this guidance system can only be accessed in reality, in the moment, by being present to real life, not through the mind. Your divine self provides answers to how to live your life through intuitions, insights, urges, motivation, inspirations, excitement, and joy. This is how you are steered through life.

Your mind will also give you answers if you let it. But like consulting an 8-ball, the answers you get from your mind might be right for some moment but not necessarily for the current one. Furthermore, if you're listening to your mind, you are likely to miss your divine self's subtle communications, which are generally wordless and experienced energetically in the body, not in the mind.

The problem with the voice in your head's advice is that it looks to conditioning for answers. Although conditioning is useful and even necessary, it isn't the place to turn for answers for how to live your life. Conditioning offers some general rules and guidelines, and that's about it: "Don't cross the street before looking both ways," "Drink plenty of water," "Don't lie on your taxes." These guidelines are only so useful.

For how to live your life, something much wiser is needed, and it exists in the same place that love exists: in the present moment. The present moment is rich! This isn't obvious from the egoic state of consciousness. It seems like there's nothing of much interest in the relatively slow moment-to-moment unfolding of life—and there isn't, to the ego.

The ego is like a child who's been spoiled with too many toys, who now finds everything boring. The mind's virtual reality is like a wonderland of toys, with anything you can imagine going on and all the drama and excitement of a rollercoaster ride. This is what TV and movies are like too. So much is going on in them that real life seems boring. So, people keep turning to their mind, TV, and movies for fun, excitement, and to feel good.

There's nothing wrong with entertainment and fun, but that isn't what life is about. Real life isn't happening in your mind or on TV or in the movies. At a certain point, you have to engage in real life. You have to *have* a life. The more time you spend in virtual reality, whether in your own mind or in someone else's, such as TV or the movies, the more dissatisfied you'll be with real life and the less functional you'll be. You have to *do* life to become good at it. Getting good at video games won't teach you how to be in life, only life can.

People want to escape into virtual reality because participating in life is more challenging than observing it. In real life, you have to make choices and take actions, and sometimes you're not happy. While you are watching TV or movies or involved in your fantasies, you get to put your problems and negative feelings on hold. For the time being, you don't have to deal with them.

When you do this habitually, you are coping with your problems and feelings through escapism rather than cultivating other, healthier ways to feel better, such as meditating, walking in nature, listening to music, watching the breeze move through the trees, or just sitting quietly. These simple activities and any number of other real-life activities will drop you into a place where insights and your inner wisdom, inspiration, creativity, and inner guidance are accessible. This is also where you can gain perspective on your so-called problems and heal your feelings.

TV, movies, and your own fantasies do nothing to help you cope with your feelings and life, and they keep you from dropping into a state of love and peace. And when you're engaged in such escapist activities, you probably aren't learning real-life skills. That means that when you return to real life, you are worse off than when you left it. All you've accomplished is reinforcing the egoic state of consciousness, which is the problem to begin with.

This is the situation more and more young people find themselves in, not to mention adults. In spending so much time in virtual reality, young people aren't learning how to cope with being in the world except by escaping it, and no one in the real world, in school or elsewhere, is teaching them an alternative.

And worse, by watching so much violence on TV, in movies, and in video games, young people are getting the message that violence is the way to cope with their problems and feelings, and no one is teaching them an alternative to that either.

Furthermore, their ego's fantasies and desires are being stoked in a way that will only cause greater disappointment and disillusionment with real life and with their own imperfections. They will never be as beautiful, brilliant, athletic, talented, or charismatic as the heroes and heroines in films, but they will suffer over wanting to be.

Subtly and not so subtly, TV and the movies are affecting children in highly negative ways—and they affected those of you who are now adults in ways you may not realize. Children and teens are, and you were, deeply conditioned by what you see on TV and the movies, much more than you probably realize.

Your society's values were and are being shaped by these stories, many of which are extremely brutal and dark. You think nothing of seeing violence, horror, murder, rape, and torture. On a daily basis, you are exposed to the worst possible experiences a human being can have.

It would be foolish to think that seeing this has no impact. Human beings are continually being conditioned by what they see and experience, and you are vicariously experiencing every manner of horror. The only way to cope with this is to become desensitized to violence and horror, and that is what's happened. That's the effect that viewing these things has had on you and is having on your children.

What has this to do with love? First of all, if you're spending time in virtual reality, in your own mind's or someone else's, you're not spending time in real relationships, which is where you learn to love. And if you are cut off from real life, you're cut off from the love of your true nature and from a rich experience of life that will fulfill you.

Many shows are much like a nightmare, with egos suffering and causing suffering. These shows reinforce the ego's viewpoint that life is scary, people are dangerous, and there's a disaster or tragedy around every corner. Doom and gloom seem to be the nature of life. It's easy to conclude that terrible things could and probably will happen to you, and that is neither true nor helpful. However, the more involved you are with the egoic mind, the more negative your reality is likely to become. Like attracts like.

These shows keep you tied to the egoic state of consciousness and reinforce the ego's beliefs about life. It's difficult to come away from most movies and TV programs without some fear and emotional trauma. Don't kid yourself: Seeing tragedy, horror, violence, and human beings behaving badly and cruelly affects you. And children, who are just forming their ideas about themselves and the world, are especially affected by this.

The problem is that the more people who are entrenched in the egoic state of consciousness, the harder it is for everyone to break free from it, and the harder it is to be content with real life and to discover the love, goodness, and beauty within humanity and yourself.

This is why there is so much negativity on your shows: Those creating them are, themselves, immersed in the ego's point of view, or they would be producing nature shows or something uplifting or educational. Then, like a virus, this state of consciousness is spread to others. The media is powerful. It's a shaper of beliefs and consciousness, not only a reflector of consciousness.

What goes on in most movies and TV shows is definitely not the Golden Rule. What you are being shown, instead, is the ego on steroids—not just an ordinary ego but often a pathological one. Because bad behavior is so common on TV and in the movies, it seems like this is just the way life is. It's what people do—they kill each other and rape and lie and cheat, right? Human beings are animals, right? In many shows, there is little acknowledgment of your divine nature, as if it doesn't exist or exists only as a weak religious impulse.

Such a ready acceptance and dismissal of violence is the first step in creating a violent society. By exposing yourselves to the worst violence and abuses through virtual reality, the door is opened in humanity's consciousness to living out these possibilities. You, yourself, may not be inclined in this direction, but there are many who are, and these shows contribute to their instability and criminal tendencies. These shows model pathological and criminal behavior, and the rest of you—your egos—are fascinated by such behavior.

Violence on TV, in the movies, and in video games is extremely unhealthy for society. It's taking more of a toll on society and on your spiritual growth than you may realize. But this is the stage humanity is at, and many other civilizations on other worlds have had to go through this stage as well.

With free will and freedom come some very bad choices, which often aren't learned from until a great deal of damage has been done. Your world will learn as others have, and in that sense, it will be okay. But since I'm writing about love, this insidious promoter and reinforcer of hate and violence must be named.

The divine self knows how to love, and if you give it half a chance, you will experience its love and guidance. But you have to give love a chance by turning off TV, movies, video games, and social media; tuning out the incessant chatter of the voice in your head; and tuning in to the subtle realm, where the Divine lives and breathes as you. Out of that realm flows love.

Chapter 4

It Is More Blessed to Give Than to Receive

Love is not so much a feeling as a doing, and that doing is essentially a giving of any number of things. When you give love to someone, you are giving them your attention, respect, openness, compassion, gentleness, curiosity, care, and kindness. These are all components of love. When you give someone love, you stop all other doing and give them yourself. In that moment, you are open and willing to listen and respond to them from a place of love and wisdom. The most valuable gift you can give someone is love, and it's a gift that benefits the giver at least as much as the receiver.

What does giving love look like? I said that love is a doing, but this doing often looks simply like receptivity and openness. The reason this is a doing is that your default is to not be open and receptive but to be the taker, to try to get something from others. It might just be attention or admiration, but that's still an attempt to get something for oneself. So, what you have to do to be with others from a place of love is to *not* do what the ego would do.

This act of not doing is a choice—a doing. To love, you have to stop doing whatever you're doing and thinking and then consciously choose to *not* do or say what is most automatic and conditioned. Then, you have to choose to do what love would have you do: Give the person in front of you your full attention, willingly, patiently, and with kindness and goodwill.

The greatest act of love is to be fully present to someone. Love receives others where they are. You allow them to be as they are, you accept them, listen to them, send love to them, and possibly at some point speak to them from your Heart, the spiritual Heart.

Did you know that love has a voice? It does. It speaks to you intuitively, and then you give it a voice. You become a mouthpiece for love, for the Divine. But this can only happen if you are in a state of love: receptive, open, kindly, and willing to be used in this way.

Many who are in their egos want to be helpful, and so they try to help from that state of consciousness. Sometimes, they're able to dip into love long enough to deliver its wisdom. But often what they offer comes from their own conditioned mind, which may not be helpful and may even be harmful. The mind just doesn't have the answers for the needs of the moment. Only the moment has these answers, and for that, you have to be in the moment, not in your head.

So many of the questions people have about their life and the things they struggle with are not the needs of the moment but a problem their own egoic mind has created unnecessarily. The solutions to these so-called problems do not and will not arise from the moment. Instead, the egoic mind will offer its solutions: The mind creates the problem and then offers its own solutions. The only true solution that could arise from the moment to such problems would be the Truth: Your own egoic mind is causing you to suffer.

The egoic mind creates all sorts of imaginary problems, and imaginary problems have no real solutions. But that is for you to discover. Many of you on the spiritual path have already discovered this. And yet, the egoic mind keeps coming up with imaginary problems, because that's what minds do.

Most of these so-called problems have to do with the ego's desires. The ego has endless desires that feel very important and true, and not having these met seems like a real problem and cause for sadness, anger, or feeling bad about oneself: "How dare life not fulfill my desires! Nothing ever works out for me. I'm just a failure."

But often, the only problem is that the ego's desires are unrealistic or not aligned with divine will and with how life is currently unfolding. The ego makes life all about itself, but maybe the time isn't right for something, or maybe it just isn't in the cards. So many things are just not under the ego's control.

The ego doesn't believe and doesn't recognize that each moment contains whatever is needed for that moment, and that whatever Life isn't providing isn't necessary at that time. There might even be a good reason, in terms of one's soul's growth, for something not being provided. Life has a plan for every individual, and the ego's desires often have little to do with that.

If the ego were able to see that it doesn't need what it thinks it needs to be happy, there would be no problem and no suffering. But that is easier said than done. The ego is in the business of wanting things that are *not* showing up in life and not wanting things that *are* showing up in life, and that is the trouble. It's a no-win situation, which is why the ego is rarely happy.

Because the ego's problems are not real problems, the only real solution is to see this. Then, letting go of the particular desire that's causing the suffering and dropping into real life, which is unfolding exactly as it needs to, is possible. Unfortunately, most people aren't ready for such wisdom and such a solution. So, they seek answers to their ego-generated problems from other egos or their own and spend their time trying to get something they think they need to be happy.

This striving to *get* rather than receiving and fully experiencing what life is offering in the moment and being grateful for that—for what *is*—is the disease that is the ego. Since there's no end to the ego's need to get more, for those in the egoic state of consciousness, life becomes all about getting. Their ongoing experience is one of never having enough and always striving for more. Their thirst is never quenched and their hunger never satisfied. This is the state most people find themselves in and the reason so many are unhappy.

If something isn't capable of making you happy for long, such as power, money, recognition, or material things, then getting more of those things is not the solution to making you happy. The answer is to go after what *is* capable of making you happy.

Love and happiness can't be found in getting things or even in getting love, at least not for long. Love and happiness belong to a state of consciousness that is only arrived at by letting go of the ego's perception that it needs to get something from outside itself to be happy, including love from others. The belief that happiness lies outside oneself is one of the lies that keeps people tied to the egoic state of consciousness. The truth is that getting what the ego wants doesn't get you what you really want: love, peace, joy, contentment, and wisdom.

You may not be aware that what you really want is love, peace, joy, contentment, and wisdom. You might be very attached to what your ego wants: You *really* want power, money, recognition, admiration, security, comfort, or beautiful material possessions. Can you see that you want *both* what the ego wants and what your true self wants? The problem is denying that you want what your true self wants and focusing exclusively on what your ego wants. As I said earlier, what you focus on, becomes magnified in your awareness. The ego's desires become bigger than life, quite literally.

What if you focused on what is more real and true than the ego's desires: love, peace, joy, contentment, and wisdom? What if those were your priority? You can still go after power, money, and the other things the ego wants, and your pursuit of these will be much more balanced and less selfishly motivated.

There are many in your world today who have both wealth and love, who attained their wealth because they stayed true to love, joy, and their innate wisdom. They allowed themselves to be guided by something higher, and that resulted in an abundant life on every level.

There are also plenty of examples of what it looks like when someone is driven solely by the ego's desires. Those individuals are not happy despite having what the ego wants. Why not learn from them? They are your teachers in this regard.

What will it be? Will you be a getter or a giver? The good news is that if you choose to be a giver, you will also "get" great blessings from life, including possibly the things the ego wants. The same is not true if you choose to be a getter. That is a lonely and unsatisfying path, as anything you do receive from life will never be enough.

Do you believe that "it is more blessed to give than to receive"? What you believe is important. The ego doesn't believe this, which is why this truth needs to be articulated. You have to be taught this because your default is to believe the opposite. The ego laughs at this teaching. The ego is a taker, not a giver. To it, giving is a sign of weakness and weakens you.

Giving makes the ego feel diminished, while amassing what it wants makes it feel good about itself. Too bad what it's trying to amass isn't love! The ego believes that there's only so much to go around, which may be true of material things but certainly not true of love.

The ego is like a miser constantly counting his stack of coins to see if he is ahead in life or behind, as if life is a game of poker or Monopoly. The ego is afraid it will end up a loser. It assesses its winning and losing with measurable things, such as the size of one's bank account, the number of awards, the size of one's house, the expensiveness of one's cars and clothing, or the number of followers on social media.

When I said, "It is easier for a camel to go through the eye of a needle than for a rich person to enter the kingdom of God," this is the kind of rich person I was referring to. What I was saying then is what I am saying here: The egoic state of consciousness, with its emphasis on accumulating money and things rather than cultivating love, makes it very difficult to discover that the "the kingdom of God is within you."

This kingdom refers to your inherent divinity—God is within you! That subtle realm where love abides is where God abides within you. That love, that goodness, *is* God's presence within you. But, of course, the miser isn't interested in that. He is too in love with other things, things that don't satisfy.

The ego definitely believes that it is more blessed to *receive* than to give, but the ego has it backwards. And when you believe something about life that isn't true, you will suffer, because that's how Life teaches you the Truth. When you don't go in the direction of love, you suffer; when you do, you don't suffer. Life is designed to teach love.

So, what is so blessed about giving? What does "it is more blessed to give than to receive" mean? This may not be obvious. The blessing in receiving and having things is obvious enough. It's a blessing to have a warm bed, food on the table, and a safe car. But as nice as these blessings are, they can't compare with the blessings received from giving, particularly giving love.

Another way of saying this is, "Man cannot live by bread alone." People will never be truly happy with only their material needs met. They need something more, and what they need isn't gained by getting more, but by giving more.

The kind of giving I'm talking about is a gift you give yourself as well as others: the gift of love. Giving love is the greatest gift, to yourself, to others, and to the world. As worthwhile as giving money or food to the poor is, if these gifts aren't given with love in your heart, then even that won't fulfill you.

By giving love, I mean giving all the things I described earlier as being part of love: attention, care, respect, compassion, gentleness, kindness, curiosity, forgiveness, and acceptance. Giving others these things aligns you with the love of your divine being and puts you in the most joyful and blessed place you can be within yourself. It puts you in contact with your divine self, with God, with goodness. True happiness lies there, true peace lies there, and wisdom.

When you give others these things—attention, care, respect, compassion, gentleness, kindness, curiosity, forgiveness, and acceptance—you return home to love. The rewards of giving love are like striking it rich because you feel rich, full, and complete within yourself.

Being present to others in this way opens the floodgates of your heart, making it possible to feel love for others and life itself, and love feels wonderful! Being present to others connects you with your heart and opens it like nothing else. That is the blessing and gift you give yourself when you choose to be lovingly present to others. The experience of this love is its own reward.

Then, from this place of love, acceptance, and wisdom, how the Divine, through you, wishes to serve others in practical ways in the world will become obvious, whether that be giving money, your time, wisdom, or something else. Connect first with the love in your Heart, and then see what love wants you to do in the world. You can become a channel of divine wisdom, inspiration, healing, and service in the world.

No amount of money can purchase the state of consciousness that is love, and no one can give you the sense of fullness, contentment, peace, and wisdom that come from this state. What you gain by giving love can only be attained by giving love. This is "the pearl beyond price." It is what you've been seeking all your lifetimes, while all along, it has been in your possession. Your capacity to love is your greatest possession.

You know how to be present to someone. You already have this skill. You practiced this skill most fervently when you first fell in love. Then, you gave your undivided attention—your love—to your beloved without reservations. You couldn't take your eyes off your beloved. You were fascinated by him or her, curious, and interested in everything about your beloved. You saw no flaws, only perfect imperfections. Everything about your beloved was adorable, endearing, and embraced. You cherished and savored every moment you were with him or her. Each moment felt so precious, full, complete, and satisfying. That is love.

That is the kind of attentiveness I'm speaking about. Can you be that attentive to whomever is in front of you, as if that person were your beloved? Mostly, this is a matter of setting aside the mind and listening with your whole body. Being present is a matter of being in your body and senses, and then dropping a little deeper to connect with the energy of love that exists in the subtle realm.

Love lives inside you energetically. You can feel it very subtly. Find that love inside yourself, focus on it, and keep some level of awareness of it when you're with others. Try to stay connected to love while you're listening to the person in front of you: your divine self in another form. Look for the goodness, Godness, in this person. Notice how he or she is like you instead of how he or she is different from you.

You are much more like others than different from them. The differences are primarily in the costume—the physical body and the personality—not deeper. Even your egos are similar, which is cause for compassion, not disdain. Look for the goodness in others and notice their ego, but don't be fooled by it. Their ego is no more who they are than your ego is who you are.

Others may not have discovered what you have about the ego and their own goodness, but they will someday. In any event, their soul's evolution is not your business. It isn't for you to judge or to even know where they are in their evolution or to feel superior because you think you have more understanding than they do. That would be the ego doing that.

Your divine self feels nothing but compassion for the suffering the ego causes within the human condition. Perhaps it is for you to relieve some of this suffering, perhaps not. You will only know the answer to this by dropping into the subtle realm, where love resides, and discovering how to move and speak from there. That is where you receive your "marching orders" from the Divine.

The ego will try to get you to march to its drummer, but you must resist that automatic tendency to comply to its wishes. You can only be of limited service to others spiritually from the egoic state of consciousness, and you can't have a truly loving relationship unless you learn to abide in the love that is your true nature and speak and move from that love.

If you aren't feeling loved or loving, then you are stuck in the egoic state of consciousness, in a number of mistaken beliefs that don't serve you. It can be helpful to examine those beliefs and discover how false they are. I've written about how to do this kind of inquiry in most of my other books.

For now, I want to emphasize that you can move out of this contracted state of consciousness by doing one fairly simple thing: sending love. It doesn't even matter who or what you send love to. The act of sending love to *anything* frees you from the prison of the egoic state of consciousness. Sending love works because you can't do this practice and be identified with your thoughts at the same time.

The practice of sending love is simply a matter of intending that love be sent somewhere and holding your attention on that for a moment. Whenever you find yourself caught up in your thoughts, for instance, try sending love to them. Then, send love to whomever or whatever is in your environment, and this will bring you more firmly into alignment with your divine self. And, of course, at any time, you can send love to those who are at a distance or those who have passed away. Sending love to those you're struggling with is a particularly powerful and healing practice. Doing this will open your heart and heal your relationship.

Sending love works because it aligns you with the divine love within you, which helps you realize that you are love and you are lovable, and that others are as well. When you are in the egoic state of consciousness, you don't feel loving because you don't feel lovable, and others don't seem very lovable either. When you feel this way, it's a sign that your heart is closed. A closed heart makes attracting love and assimilating any love you do receive from others difficult. Sending love is a remedy for this.

One of the rewards of giving love is that you feel good about yourself. The Catch-22 is that if you don't love yourself, then being loving toward others is difficult. Somehow, this vicious cycle has to be broken, and a practice of consciously choosing to send love to others can do that, even if at first you aren't experiencing love when you do this practice.

The more you practice sending love, the more you feel worthy of receiving love. And the more worthy of love you feel, the easier it is to give love. And the more you give love, the more people love you and want to support you in various ways.

What you put out into the world is returned to you. If you put love out into the world, you'll receive love and so much more back. "Seek first the kingdom of God, and all else will be added to you." Give love, and all else will be given to you.

What people discover when they give love is that it isn't receiving love and the other benefits that love draws to them that makes them happy as much as the act of giving love. This is an amazing discovery! Giving is where the "juice," the joy, is. Giving is what feels good. What a surprise!

The ego believes the opposite of the Truth, so it really shouldn't be a surprise to discover that the truth is the opposite of what the ego believes! This is why "the truth will set you free." It sets you free from the ego.

So, here is how to do the practice of sending love. This practice may seem esoteric, but it is absolutely something anyone can do. To send love:

❖ Think of a person, pet or other animal, plant, or thing you want to send love to. Or notice a thought, feeling, or sensation that you might send love to.

❖ Then, connect with the subtle experience of love within your being.

❖ Next, intend that love be sent to whatever you've chosen to send love to and hold your attention on this intention for a moment.

❖ Imagine or feel the love energetically flowing from you to whatever you've chosen to send love to for a few minutes.

The purpose of sending love is to transform your consciousness and that of others. The effect that sending love has on your own consciousness will affect everything around you, and sending love specifically to someone else affects that person directly. Energy follows thought. It goes wherever you intend it to go. If you send love to someone, his or her energy body registers that, even at a distance.

Human beings are made of energy, and you are affected by each other's energy in beneficial and not so beneficial ways, whether you are conscious of that or not. Most people aren't sending a high vibration of energy to others—love—but something more like the energy of lack, fear, or anger.

Fortunately, the energy of love can be consciously directed to others by you for the good of all if you intend that.

Buddhists have a wonderful practice of sending love to others by reciting "May all beings be happy" and variations of this. Wishing others well is a powerful prayer. Doing this aligns you with your divine self and with love and uplifts others. Feel free to make up your own prayers or statements of this nature and use them.

Giving love to others by sending them love, wishing them well, or praying for them makes you happy and makes it easier for others to be happy too. When you give love in these ways, you are summoning guiding forces to help and protect others, and they come forward to do this. Your good intentions matter, not only to your state of consciousness, but to others. Your goodwill—love—is an actual force in the world. You can be either a force that is in service to love or one that works against love. You decide. Please choose to make this a better world.

Chapter 5

Love God with All Your Heart

"Love the Lord your God with all your heart and with all your soul and with all your mind. This is the first and greatest Commandment." Any teaching about love must include loving God. What does it mean to love God with all your heart? Why would you or should you love God? And what if you don't? This is what I'd like to explore with you in this chapter.

There is a reason that this is the first and greatest Commandment. Without a love for God, it is difficult to love. Loving God is primary to love and to existence. Loving God is synonymous to loving life. How could you not love God and still love life, what God has created and the life God has given you? If you don't love God, it would only be because you find it difficult to love your mistaken idea of God, and who could blame you?

That is the problem for many, who have come to see God as a religious prop, a mythological character, or a fearsome and punishing force. Many have walked away from religion altogether because the God depicted by religion, in so many cases, doesn't seem loving and fair. That God is too much like you: cruel, wrathful, and punishing. But you were made in

God's image, not the other way around, and God does not have an ego. God is love and everything that entails.

In your heart, you know that love is essential and your reason for being, and when religions don't reflect this deep knowing and don't make sense in other ways, many feel they have to walk away. Some of you find your way back to a philosophy that includes God as a loving force and some do not. Those who don't are challenged to find a way to make sense of life and to love life. And those who continue to believe unloving religious ideas continue to suffer as a result of those beliefs. They are imprisoned in a false mindset, as they believe they've already found the truth.

Loving God—loving love—is the antidote to the ego's negative beliefs and ways. The ego is anti-love because the ego doesn't make love a priority. The ego has other gods than love. The problem with this is that life doesn't go well when you make other things more important than love in your life, when you worship what the ego worships. Your values inform your choices, and when your values are off, your choices will be. To misunderstand life is to suffer, while understanding the meaning and purpose of life enables you to love life.

What you believe about God is very important. I've spent a good deal of time on this subject in another book called *All Grace,* so I won't go into as much detail here, but one thing must be understood: God is good, life is good, and you are good. The fact that life on earth can be difficult and that you've been given the challenge of having an ego doesn't negate this basic truth about life.

What you believe about God is important because it determines how you feel inside. If you believe that God and life are good and that love is behind life, you will relax and allow yourself to experience that love and goodness—your own divine nature. On the other hand, if you believe that God doesn't exist or that God is a punishing force, or some other false belief, then all that's left to guide you is your default programming.

Following your egoic programming will result in negative feelings, actions not in keeping with Thy will, and a lack of contact with your own loving nature. What you believe about God and about life determines the state of consciousness you abide in, and your state of consciousness determines your experience of life, the actions you take, and what you attract to you.

Religion serves to the extent that people take away the message that love is all-important and they ignore the mistaken messages, the ones that are anti-love, such as the idea that your essential nature is sinful, or that some are punished eternally in Hell, or that accepting me as your savior is the only way to eternal life, which some use as an excuse to not apply themselves to following the prescription of love that I gave you.

Most of you have misunderstandings about God and about life that distort your perceptions of life and prevent you from the joy and love that are possible. That is not to say that you don't have some fun and enjoyment in the egoic state of consciousness. You do, when you do things the ego enjoys and when the ego is getting what it wants, which is the compensation for having an ego.

But before long, the voice in your head is back to tormenting you and pushing you to strive harder to try to make life be the way your ego wants it to be. Having an ego is exhausting, and for many, escapist activities are the only way to get a brief respite from the stress caused by the voice in their head.

"If only I could get rid of the voice in my head," you may think. But that is the tricky ego thinking that very thought. The Divine in you doesn't need or wish for the ego to go away. It accepts the voice in the head as part of life and willingly lives with it, just as you accept the stars or anything else you can't do anything about.

What good would it do, anyway, to not accept something you can't do anything about? And yet, that is the situation in which people find themselves much of the time, when they listen to the voice in their head and believe it to be their voice and what they believe and want.

If you observe this voice, you'll notice that it's unhappy with life most of the time. It's complaining, longing for something else, imagining what it would be like to have what it wants, and plotting to make things different. It's comparing something in the present to the past and to its fantasies, comparing you with others, and coming up with suggestions for improvements. That is its job, you could say.

But that isn't a good formula for how to live your life. Life is not about pushing for improvements, certainly not improvements designed by the ego. Improvements naturally come out of the flow, since change and evolution are built into life. Rather, life is about living: about experiencing what *is*. Having an ego is like being offered a feast and instead of wholeheartedly partaking in the feast, you evaluate it, plan for another feast, compare it to a feast you once had or heard of, fantasize about a better feast, and take pictures of the feast.

This is the ego's world. When you are involved with the voice in your head, you aren't living in reality. You are living in "what ifs" and "I wants" and "I don't likes," not in a state of love. What you experience instead of real life and love are evaluations, judgments, and thoughts about the past and future, and those only take you away from love and farther into your desires and fears. In the egoic state of consciousness, you experience your thoughts instead of reality, without even realizing that this is what's going on.

While you're busy thinking, life is happening, and you missed it. Yes, you missed something. The ego thinks nothing is going on in the here and now, so it isn't concerned about missing something. But the mind, the ego, can't experience reality; it can only think about reality. The voice in your head keeps you involved with it and avoids reality by making up stories and forming opinions. These stories and opinions are *its* reality.

Stop a moment, and really see this: The mind isn't what experiences reality—your *being,* your divine self, does. Your divine self is right here, right now, reading or listening to this. Your divine self isn't something abstract or distant from your life! It is the consciousness that is experiencing your life. It is what is aware of whatever you're aware of. It's what is looking out of your eyes.

However, your experience of life gets co-opted by thoughts *about* experience. Your default causes you to trade in real life for thoughts about real life. But once you drop out of thought, the experience of real life is right there, waiting for you!

You experience real life and the love of your divine nature whenever you're having fun, playing, and losing yourself in some game, activity, or creative project. This is what I meant when I said, "Unless you change and become like little children, you will never enter the kingdom of heaven."

Little children have yet to develop a strong sense of self and ego, and easily lose themselves in play. They live in the present moment, and so, they enjoy life. They are in awe of life. They laugh and love and have fun. They experience the joy and delight of their true nature more easily than adults. The kingdom I was speaking about is the kingdom of your divine self, the kingdom of love: reality.

Activities you enjoy, especially ones that involve being fully in your body and senses, such as playing an instrument or dancing, are fun and make you happy because, like little children, you've stepped into real life and stopped thinking about your life, what you like, what you believe, and what you want. The reward for being involved in real life is fun and delight, although the ego may have a different definition of fun.

The ego is looking to feel high about itself. To the ego, doing things that make it feel good about itself and improve its self-image is fun. It likes to win games, it likes to win money, it likes to win! To the ego, winning is fun. The ego even likes working out because it imagines being admired for having a strong and attractive body. The ego thinks shopping is fun for the same reason—getting nice, new things is good for one's self-image. Eating is also really fun, which isn't so good for the self-image, but indulging in pleasures is another of the ego's favorite pastimes.

When you're in touch with your divine self, any moment has the potential to be fun, including working out and things that generally wouldn't be considered fun. The joy of being in the present moment is something most people have to discover for themselves by being present long enough. Everyone has brief moments of being present, but few live in this state of consciousness or even realize this is possible or how to make this possible.

The fun of being in the present moment is more like contentment, completeness, joy, peace, awe, wonder, delight, and a love for life. It's a sense of expansion, wholeness, connectedness, and gratitude for the gift of existence and all that entails. What more could you ask for?

Being fully in the present moment has a feeling of richness and satisfaction that is missing in the egoic state of consciousness. The egoic state is like eating fast food: No matter how much you eat, you still don't feel really good or satisfied. That's because your soul can only be fed in the here and now. Only love satisfies, and that is as it is meant to be. That's how life shows you what is true, important, and of value.

Being present is not a mystical experience or difficult to attain. Being present is a very ordinary and simple state, one you experience throughout your day whenever you aren't lost in thought. However, most people don't think much of this state when they do experience it because they don't stay in it long enough to "taste" it.

Tasting is a good metaphor for this: If you take a bite of the most delicious dessert and swallow it right away, you miss the full experience of it. Likewise, if you dip into the present moment only briefly, you miss the full experience of it. You may think you experienced it, but you didn't. You only dipped your toe in, and that isn't the same as swimming in the ocean, to use another metaphor.

The problem is that if you don't know what you're missing by being lost in thought, you won't choose to be present; you won't choose against the default. You need to experience the beauty, contentment, and joy of the present moment long enough to want to stay there.

This is why meditation and other spiritual practices that teach you to be present are so necessary. They show you that another state of consciousness is possible, and they teach you how to shift into that state and stay there. With a practice of meditation, you'll discover what you are missing by not being present and begin to want that more than your thoughts. In this way, attachment to the voice in your head is loosened.

A practice of meditation trains you to be in the present moment longer and longer. Eventually, you won't want to return to the old way of being—of being lost in thoughts about *me, myself, and I*. It feels so good to lose the "I." When you do, you discover that you never needed this "I" to live your life. You see that it is a pretend self. All along, your true self has been who you really are, but it allowed you to pretend that you were a fearful, limited self.

Losing your sense of "I," the false self, and all its stories, fears, and desires is the goal of the spiritual path. What you gain when you lose the false self is your true self and its peace, joy, and love. It's a good tradeoff!

This shift from thinking of yourself as the false self to knowing yourself as the true self and living as that is called awakening. You awaken out of the ego into the realization of who you essentially are. Then, you can begin to live more as I did. This is a shift from living in your head to living in the present moment, from living in a made-up reality to living in reality. And reality is good! It is of God, of love, and so are you.

"Love the Lord your God with all your heart and with all your soul and with all your mind" means love, love: Love the love that is within you. Love the goodness, the Godness, that is within you. To love God means to honor love and goodness and follow love and goodness. When you love something with all your heart and all your soul and all your mind, you give it your attention, you are devoted to it, you put it above all else, you worship it, you follow it. Worship love! Follow love!

There is no God in the sky that you should worship. That would be a false idol. Many today are too sophisticated and rational to believe that God is a human-like being sitting on a throne in the sky. And if those who do believe this weren't threatened by the fear of Hell into believing this, they surely wouldn't believe this either. Love God doesn't mean worship your idea of God. It means put love above all else in all you say and do, since God *is* love.

If you do this, you will be happy and you will fulfill all the Commandments. That is why this is the first and greatest of all Commandments. Your relationship with God is the primary relationship. If you are in right relationship to God—to love—then you will be in right relationship with all of life. *Love* is the first and greatest Commandment: Honor love above all else.

This is impossible from the egoic state of consciousness. That is why you must find your way back to love from this fearful and illegitimate state. The egoic state of consciousness is illegitimate; it is not in accordance with divine law. It is outside of Truth. Your journey as a spiritual being is to find your way back to love from this state that is divorced from love.

The egoic state of consciousness is a state of being lost, in the same way that the prodigal son, who was caught up in the grasping and cravings of the ego, was lost. Like the prodigal son's adventure, your spiritual journey on earth is a story of redemption: God, who incarnates as you, loses Himself/Herself in matter, in the egoic state of consciousness, only to return to His/Her original state of love all the wiser.

God incarnates in human form to have the experience of being human and having an ego. Christians mistakenly believe that I am the only one who incarnated as God, the only son of God, but every single human being is an incarnation of God. You are all sons and daughters of God, engaged in discovering the love at your core and finding your way back Home.

Love is all there is. There is only God, and God is love. Then, God created a reality in which God could be divorced from love to experience what that would be like. The ego is what makes it possible for God to be lost to love and have any number of experiences that God couldn't have had otherwise. But God also endowed human beings with an internal guidance system so that God couldn't get lost forever and a failsafe device that would ensure that God would wake up at some point and remember His/Her own divine nature.

God is alive in you! Can you feel this? Can you feel God's divine presence within you? It's not so mysterious, really. It is your kindness, compassion, peace, joy, love, wisdom, courage, inner strength, inspiration, brilliance, and adoration of God. That which is seeking God, which loves God, is God itself! And what you are seeking, you already are!

You are waking up to this fact. You don't have to become anything. You already are it. You are becoming aware that you are already God. And then, the task is to be that in the world, as a human being. For this, I am a model for you, but I'm not the only one who is a model for love and enlightenment.

I have already given you one key for waking up to your divine self, and that is meditation. Another very powerful practice is prayer: Pray for assistance in waking up and living in love. Declare your allegiance to goodness and love, and spiritual forces will come forward to support you in that. These are prayers that will always be answered. On the other hand, the ego's prayers for its desires to be met may or may not be answered, and having them be met may or may not be beneficial.

Pray for things that are unquestionably beneficial: Pray for greater love, acceptance, compassion, strength, courage, growth, and the ability to forgive others and let go of the past. Pray to be of greater service to others and for help in fulfilling your life purpose. Pray for these things, and your prayers will always be answered.

Those who are guiding humanity are waiting for you to ask for their help in awakening and living in love. Although you aren't completely in control of when and how you awaken to your divine nature, your intention and commitment are important factors in facilitating and hastening your awakening or slowing it down if you lack that intention and commitment.

Spiritual forces honor whatever you intend and offer extra assistance only when you show them you are ready to receive it. One of the ways to demonstrate your readiness is to ask them for their help. The specific words you use are not important. What matters is what's in your heart. Spiritual forces respond to your sincere intention, your longing, and your actions, which signal your level of commitment.

Praying will help you develop a relationship with God and strengthen your belief in guiding forces. This is important because it opens the door to further benefits from nonphysical forces. They *do* exist, and they exist to help you. The more you realize this, the more you can know that God is good, that the intelligence behind life is good.

I like to refer to God as the intelligence behind all life or the life force within all life because it helps you to understand that God doesn't exist as a separate entity. As children, most of you were taught that "God created Man in His own image," so you imagined a God who looks like you. However, what is meant by this is that human beings have God's divine qualities and are inherently good and of love.

God is not at all like a human being. By the way, you are not actually human either! You are God playing at being a human being. Human beings are only one form that God takes on. God is an unimaginable force and intelligence, which is perhaps why human beings have needed to see God as something they can relate to. And that's fine.

It's fine to talk to God as if God were a good parent, but please understand that this is not actually the case. The trouble with imagining that God is similar to a human being is that God may also be assumed to have the negative propensities of human beings, and nothing could be farther from the truth.

For instance, God would never punish what God has created. That would be God punishing Himself/Herself, and what good could come of that? Punishment is a crude and cruel means of teaching, which imprisons, not elevates. The suffering you experience in life is not punishment for any so-called sins but something you generate within yourselves by incorrect thinking, by egoic thinking.

God is so good and loving that God has given you—Himself/Herself—a way out of suffering, and that is to see the truth about life. The truth is that the programming you've been given is faulty, and *it* is the source of your suffering, not anything about life itself.

Life is beautiful, wonderful, and although challenging, a precious gift, which your soul has chosen to experience for any number of reasons. The reasons in general are for your growth and evolution and for returning to love. The suffering of the egoic state of consciousness motivates you to discover how not to suffer, and the answer to that is love!

So please, love God and develop a relationship with God and with the helping forces God has put in place for you. They are individuated enough for you to relate to and speak to. By all means, call upon them, and they will guide you on your way Home.

Chapter 6

As You Sow, so Shall You Reap

This chapter's title, "As you sow, so shall you reap," represents a basic spiritual truth that has been taught throughout the ages. Your actions and speech, which stem from your thoughts, have certain consequences and cause certain reactions from others, often quite immediately. This relates to the law of karma: What you put out into the world comes back to you. What you do to others, they are likely to do back to you, whether that deed is a kind one or an unkind one.

As a result, it's best to behave toward others as you would like others to behave toward you. "Judge not, and ye shall not be judged; condemn not, and ye shall not be condemned; forgive, and ye shall be forgiven; give, and it shall be given unto you." We are back to the Golden Rule: "Do unto others as you would have them do unto you."

The reason for the Golden Rule is the law of karma. It's why adhering to the Golden Rule is important. Following the Golden Rule leads to good results, and not following it leads to the opposite. What you think, say, and do is important and has consequences, if not immediately then at some point. The law of karma teaches this and, more essentially, teaches love.

The law of karma teaches people how to behave and how not to behave, and the guiding force behind that is love. Karma is the Great Teacher and a shaper of one's destiny. Your behavior shapes your destiny—what you are likely to experience, particularly from others.

Life is not haphazard but operates according to spiritual law: There are consequences for your thoughts, words, and deeds. The law of karma is the foundation of morality and ethical behavior. That certain actions reap good results and others reap bad ones is consistent throughout history and cultures. This law, like all natural laws, is immutable.

However, the workings of the law of karma are not always obvious, since the results or reactions that you have "sown" don't necessarily appear immediately, or even within the same lifetime, or in a form that you would recognize. So, it often seems that those who harm others get away with their injustices and those who adhere to morality are not always rewarded.

Nevertheless, goodness is its own reward, and those who behave badly or harm others are suffering as they do this. It hurts to be divorced from love, and that suffering is a potential deterrent to bad behavior if one pays attention to such guidance signals.

Morality is built into life through the law of karma. Karma teaches by guiding you away from meanness, pettiness, selfishness, unkindness, impatience, carelessness, and every other negative quality you can think of. And it teaches by guiding you toward virtuous behavior, which is essentially based on love: kindness, forgiveness, compassion, patience, acceptance, tolerance, humility, generosity, and so forth.

The thing is, you know what is "naughty" and what is "nice;" you know what is virtuous and what is not. Why is this? Were you born knowing this, or did you learn this? The answer is that everyone is born good and with a desire to be good and born knowing what is good. People are also born with an inner compass that points them toward goodness, toward love, moment to moment. However, this compass is ignored or overridden to one extent or another by one's ego or by having experienced abuse from other egos.

This moral compass guides you moment to moment by signaling you energetically. By noting how your body feels energetically, you can know when you are behaving badly and when you aren't. When you engage in unloving behavior, you experience a contraction of your energy, just as you feel a relaxation of your energy when you are aligned with love.

The feeling of "ahhh" represents the sense of expansion, relaxation, and peace that comes with no longer being in the ego's grip. What a relief! The opposite experience of tenseness and tightness represents the egoic state of consciousness. This moment-to-moment guidance system tells you what you are aligned with and what you are putting out into the world.

You also have an intuitive guidance system, which is insightful rather than energetic. Throughout your day, your divine self communicates with you, although many aren't aware of those communications because their attention is on the voice in their head. If your mind is silent or you aren't engaged with it, you'll notice these communications, or intuitions, which feel like a download, a sudden knowing, or an "ah-ha!" Moment to moment, you are given the insights, inspiration, creative ideas, motivation, reminders, warnings, wisdom, or information you need.

Everyone is being guided toward goodness, love, and fulfilling their life purpose. You are being guided toward a happy life! These intuitive communications are often called the Holy Spirit or the "still, small voice within." Others attribute them to guardian angels. Such "angels" are not an imagination but a real phenomenon. Metaphysical interventions from angelic and other nonphysical beings are a fact of life and evident to those who are psychically sensitive.

This loving guidance as well as other more tangible forms of help is grace. Throughout this frequently difficult human life, you are given so much grace, although you may not always recognize Grace's helping hand. Grace comes not only in the form of insights, guidance, and creative inspiration, but also as love, healing, helpful people, opportunities, gifts, and anything else you may need to manage your challenges and learn from them.

Life can be a beautiful experience despite the challenges, and even because of them, as challenges lend a richness and depth to life if you are able to gain in courage, compassion, patience, acceptance, and love as a result of them. This is as it is meant to be. Your challenges are not meant to turn you into victims but heroes. You are meant to become better human beings as a result of them—more aligned with your divinity. Challenges are meant to point you toward Home and develop the qualities you need to become a Christed individual. You are being forged in this crucible of life.

Life makes you strong. If your challenges are not having that effect, you need to look inside and discover how you are preventing this. What beliefs are you holding that keep you from becoming the hero of your life? Who are you blaming for your difficulties? The hero learns and grows from difficulties. What are you telling yourself that prevents you from accepting or learning from whatever you are experiencing? This is your spiritual work.

Some of your difficulties are created by karma: by your own thoughts, words, and deeds. How might you have created, drawn to you, or allowed the challenging situation you find yourself in? What was your role in it? How might you learn from it?

Other difficulties are chosen by the soul before life or in the midst of life for growth. It's always best to assume that you're having the right experience, either one you need for karmic reasons or for your soul's growth. Assuming that will help you accept your circumstances. From there, you can begin to take positive steps to remedy the situation and learn from it.

Acceptance is always possible because your divine self is always accepting. What doesn't accept a situation is the ego. Just see that and turn away from the ego's nonacceptance. Find acceptance in your heart as best you can, and don't get stuck in the ego's nonacceptance. That is a dead end. Not accepting something makes it impossible to do something about it, while acceptance frees you to move forward. Acceptance is the first step in healing and changing something you don't like.

To succeed in life in the truest sense of the word, you have to be strong. What I mean by this is that you must not fall prey to negativity, victimization, self-pity, anger, resentment, hatred, revenge, or fear. These are the ego's responses to difficulties, and they are dysfunctional. They paralyze you or create karma, which will only result in more bad feelings and more difficulties.

Many find themselves in a negative spiral of their own making: Something bad happens, and they react negatively instead of as a hero might. Then, that creates more negativity, and that creates even more negativity. Coming out of that negative spiral can be hard because life really seems to be against you. You really believe your ego's version of things, when all along you created the situation with your own negativity. The lesson is to realize this.

The farther into negativity you go, the more difficult it is to discover this because your bad experiences have reinforced your ego's viewpoint. Your false perceptions have become self-fulfilling prophecies, but you don't realize that, and you may not be open to seeing that. Life is difficult, indeed, under these circumstances.

Nonacceptance and blame keep you submerged in negativity. As long as you blame others for your feelings and situation, you won't learn your lessons, and you won't become the hero of your life. Blame prevents you from taking responsibility for what you have created or at least co-created. Once you see your responsibility in this, you can begin to make better choices, but if you don't, why would you choose differently?

Nonacceptance and blame result in feeling victimized, and that's a very stuck place. The ego actually likes being the victim. It feels self-righteous in that role and doesn't want to let that go. Being a martyr has a certain appeal. To free yourself, you must find that which is within you that wants freedom from this suffering and wants love and peace more than it wants to play the martyr.

The courage and wisdom are there within you to draw upon if you look for them and are willing to transform your experience. But you have to be willing to see that you played a role in creating that situation, if only by allowing yourself to become a victim. You have to take some responsibility for the situation.

So, let's talk about responsibility. The bad news is that you are responsible for your inner experience of life and for the feelings and actions that flow from that. The good news is that, since you are responsible for this, you also have the means for changing this if you don't like the results.

Here is how this works: You have a thought, which you aren't responsible for, since you didn't cause that initial thought to arise. However, you do have the choice to believe that thought or not, the choice to think more of those thoughts or not, and the choice to act on those thoughts or not. These are choices you *are* responsible for if you have enough self-awareness to realize this.

This awareness develops as one advances spiritually. Before that, you are largely at the mercy of your programming. But even then, you are always free to choose against the programming; no one is forcing you to follow your programming.

Your thoughts create your inner reality, or what I like to call your inner climate: what the weather inside is like. Is it sunny, cloudy, stormy, cold, hot, or calm? Positive thoughts create positive feelings, while negative thoughts create negative feelings. The beliefs and stories you hold cause you to feel the way you do. Other people don't make you feel bad or feel anything; you make yourself feel bad.

This is important to see because seeing this empowers you to create a different inner reality if you don't like how you feel. You can pick and choose what thoughts you will hold as true and which ones you will discard. Most of the ego's thoughts are negative and can be discarded. The positive thoughts in your mind are more likely from a positive upbringing or any work you've done on yourself to overcome the negative mind.

What you eventually see once you spend some time examining the voice in your head is that you don't need to live by any of those thoughts, except the few true ones. For the most part, the voice in your head is like "a sounding brass or a clanging cymbal." It is empty of Truth, empty of love and wisdom. The ideal inner climate is the result of a quiet mind, a mind that is no longer chattering and being listened to.

Your inner climate has a vibration that others feel subtly. From that climate come feelings, speech, and actions, whose effect on others is more obvious. If what you're putting out in the world is negative, then what you are likely to get back or attract will be negative. Like attracts like, and negativity repels positivity. If you're putting out negativity, you'll not only attract negativity but repel positivity.

It's no wonder that some experience people and life in general as negative, threatening, and difficult, while others experience people and life as positive, helpful, and not overwhelmingly difficult. Your inner state determines your experience of others and the world, and draws to you people and events that reflect your inner state and repel the opposite. A positive inner state attracts positivity and repels negativity, while a negative inner state attracts negativity and repels positivity. This is what is meant by the phrase "you create your reality."

However, something else is in play in life besides what you are creating. There's a bigger hand in life than yours: Grace, which is administered by spiritual forces. Spiritual forces are working on your soul's behalf to bring about your lessons and soul's plan. They arrange circumstances to help you learn and accomplish what you came to earth to learn and accomplish. Those circumstances are not created by you. So, although you are responsible for much of what you experience, the hand of Grace is bringing things into your life and taking things away according to what is needed to accomplish your life purpose and further your soul's evolution.

Grace works within the life that you are creating with your free will. For instance, if you are going to medical school to become a doctor, then Grace will work its lessons into your life within that setting. And if completing medical school would interfere with your soul's plan, then Grace will create circumstances that will block that direction for you. Somehow, Grace will steer you in another direction.

I can't emphasize enough that both karma and Grace are loving forces. Their purpose is never to punish but to teach and guide. The sometimes unpleasant results of karma and Grace are not proof that life isn't good or benevolent. The unpleasantness is the result of having an ego that bucks life at every turn. The ego doesn't like much of what goes on in life. Many of the circumstances or changes that karma or Grace bring about in one's life are not objectively bad; the ego just sees them that way.

For instance, being blocked in pursuing your career as a doctor might seem like a calamity, when it's a blessing in disguise because you wouldn't have been happy as a doctor. Many of the changes and even challenges in one's life are blessings in disguise. It's just that the ego doesn't recognize them as blessings or even recognize the blessings that aren't disguised!

The ego is so resistant to change and to anything that doesn't fit its narrow picture of how life should look that it's bound to be frequently upset and disappointed. Only a small range of possibilities is acceptable to the ego at any one time. The ego thinks it knows how life should go, and if it doesn't go that way, it's unhappy. The ego isn't open-minded or flexible, and it often doesn't recognize the opportunities that life does present. Meanwhile, life is full of possibilities that the ego never dreamed of that could make one happy and probably happier than what the ego had in mind.

"Life is what happens when you're busy making other plans," as John Lennon so wisely said. The egoic mind plans, but life has its own plan, and when the ego's plan and life's don't coincide, people suffer. But maybe life had a better plan. In fact, you can trust that life does have a better plan than anything your mind could come up with.

The egoic mind is not equipped to plan your life, and yet, it tries to. It pretends to be able to run your life, but it isn't wise enough to do this. It isn't in touch with what *is* running your life, so that's a problem. So much suffering is caused by assuming that you know what's best for you. But when this *you* is the ego, the false self, then that guidance will be false.

There is a *you* that does know what's best for you, but it isn't accessed through thought. That *you* communicates with you through the spiritual Heart, through intuition, which is very different from the voice in your head. For one thing, the spiritual Heart communicates in its own time, so you won't receive answers from it whenever you want. Its insights and guidance arise in their own time.

Timing is everything, which is something the ego doesn't appreciate. The ego wants everything *now*. But "for everything there is a season and a time for every purpose under heaven." Life happens on its own beautiful and perfect timetable. Just because the ego doesn't see that timetable as perfect doesn't alter that fact.

Assuming things like this that aren't true is another way that the ego's perceptions create unnecessary suffering. It declares: "This shouldn't be happening!" or "This needs to happen now!" But it's wrong. Whatever is happening *should* be happening, because it *is*. And whatever isn't happening shouldn't be happening, because it *isn't*.

There is a perfect wisdom in whatever *is,* a perfect unfolding, and it can be no other way than as it is—for now. All of life conspired for things to be as they are in any moment, and that cannot be changed, and this must be accepted. What *is,* is what everyone involved needs to experience for the time being, and it's best to see it this way.

An unimaginable intelligence is steering your life and everyone else's. This is one of the important lessons of life, which isn't learned until you are nearly ready to graduate from this plane of existence. You really can "let go and let God," because you are in good hands. But you won't discover this until you do let go, and some people never do. They keep turning to the voice in their head for direction, since it seems like there's nowhere else to turn. But once you turn away from this voice, you discover that something else is in charge, and the voice in your head is only pretending to know what it's doing.

The thing is, life happens whether you are listening to the voice in your head or not. The voice in your head is an added factor in the unfolding of life, a complicating factor that the Divine has to work around or work with. Once the voice in your head is out of the picture, the Divine can work unencumbered in your life. It doesn't have to find ways to stop you or steer you; it can just guide you intuitively.

There are lots of people who are already living this way. Their experience of life is one of ease, grace, support, gentleness, simplicity, beauty, love, and peace. This sounds good, doesn't it? Everyone wants to feel this way. Everyone is the same in this way and in every other way that really counts.

Everyone wants to be happy, everyone wants to live in peace, and everyone wants to love and be loved. These are universal desires. They have been implanted in you by God.

These are not things the ego wants, however, at least not more than the other things it wants.

Human beings have conflicting desires. What the ego wants often makes it difficult to experience the joy, peace, and love of your divine self. For instance, if your ego is driven toward making lots of money, the fast-paced, egoic lifestyle that often goes with making lots of money may make it difficult to experience the joy, peace, and love of your true nature.

The divine self often allows the ego's desires and drives to win out. It allows people to choose what their ego wants until they no longer want that, unless that choice interferes with their soul's plan. That is the setup: Follow your egoic programming and have those lessons and experiences. Then, once you've had your fill of the egoic state of consciousness and its suffering, you'll be ready for and open to another way of being in life.

Fortunately, there *is* a better way. There's a time for everything, and the time eventually comes for you to discover what it's like to no longer be at the mercy of your programming and to pursue the deeper desires of your divine self.

This shift is monumental in one's life. When this happens, not everything in your life necessarily changes, but your orientation changes. Instead of being oriented toward the voice in your head, your attention goes to the present moment, to what's coming out of the flow. That is the alternative to listening to the voice in your head.

Life is coming out of the now, and the life that you are meant to have is directed and steered by drives, urges, inspiration, ideas, motivation, excitement, and joy. When you follow these drives and this joy, you will be happy, which is God's intention. All along, God has been waiting for you to say yes to the life that has been planned for you, which is unfolding moment to moment.

To the extent that you are aligned with that perfect unfolding, you will be happy and fulfilled. To the extent that you aren't, you won't be. Life is good! What it has in store for every individual is good. Even your most difficult challenges were chosen by your soul as a means to grow quickly or in ways that you could not have otherwise grown.

Before closing this chapter, I want to emphasize one last time that the reason most people's lives are so difficult is not because life is difficult or needs to be difficult, but because people are following the wrong master. They're allowing their programming to run their lives. That wouldn't be a problem if the programming were kind, accepting, compassionate, and wise, but the programming is the opposite of this. And when you are the opposite of kind, accepting, compassionate, and wise, your life will not go well, because it's not supposed to.

The purpose of life is to teach you to be loving, while the ego is pulling you in the opposite direction. You learn the value of love by doing the opposite of love, and in that sense, the ego serves: You reap what you sow, and it isn't pretty.

But there's a much easier way to live. You can bypass the negative lessons of the ego now and go straight to love. You've had enough of the ego's lessons and difficult experiences. Just choose love, and see what happens. Do the opposite of what the ego does.

I'll share one more piece of advice about the path of love. Don't wait until you feel love to give love. Give love first! No matter how bad you feel, you can always choose to give love, and your inner state will change. The ego makes you feel bad about yourself, but you don't have to settle for that. You can change your inner state by expressing your goodness, your Godness, in some way.

When you need to, do what you can to change your inner state: Express your gratitude, give someone a compliment, tell someone what you appreciate about him or her, smile, make someone laugh, do something nice for someone, write someone a loving note, give someone your full attention, sing a song about love, read something inspiring, pray for the well-being of others, apologize if you need to, surrender your thoughts about others, and let others be as they are.

Doing these things takes very little time and energy and costs nothing, but reaps great benefits for yourself and others. Let these be your new habits. Doing these things regularly will plant you firmly on the path of love and keep you there.

And don't forget to pray for our help. We can help you remain strong, we can remind you to be loving, and we can clear negative influences from your energy field. Allow us to send love to you and be your companions on the path of love.

Chapter 7

The Way and the Truth and the Life

When I said, "I am the Way and the Truth and the Life," I was stating the Truth: God, or the force of love that animates all life, is the way and the Truth and the life. I was not speaking personally about myself as Jesus. What I meant is that *love* is the way to live, *love* is the Truth, and *love* is the way to eternal life, not in the sense of heaven, but as a way to know yourself as the eternal being that you are. When you know yourself as love, you know yourself as God.

This God-force, the "I am," that is within me is the same God-force that is within you. The consciousness that is within me is also within you. God is the same in everyone, and God's name is Love.

I have already said quite a bit about love being the way to live your life. But there's an important point I want to add: Love is the *only* way. There is only one way, and that way is love. "No one comes to the Father but through me," meaning through love.

Love is a narrow path and a path less-trodden. Those who take this path must be willing to be different and break away from the pack, to go their own way and follow what's true for them, with a small "t," while also following the Truth with a capital "T."

The ego's path is the path of least resistance. It's easy, broad, and well-populated, but it won't get you there. That path takes you in the wrong direction. As a result, it is the path of suffering. No matter how successful, how wealthy, how beautiful, or how admired you are, that path won't get you where you want to go and where you're meant to go. "For what shall it profit a man if he gain the whole world and suffer the loss of his soul?"

There is no other meaningful path than love. Why am I emphasizing this? Because choosing love is the last thing the ego wants to do. Love is the last path the ego will take, so as long as you remain loyal to the ego, you won't choose love's path. As long as you believe that your thoughts are true, necessary, and interesting, you will remain on the ego's path. That isn't a problem, as the soul is okay with you taking as long as you choose before you see the Truth. But it *is* a problem if you long for a happier and more fulfilled life than the one you're having.

The reason love needs to be emphasized at all is because love is somewhat of a dirty word to the ego. To it, love seems weak, uncool, sappy, goody-two-shoes, emotional, girly, babyish, unrealistic, idealistic. Love is also too much trouble. Love isn't easy. It requires effort, and that is the real problem. Following the programming is easy, particularly because everyone is doing that.

What if you were to make love important when no one you know is doing that? What will others think of you? What will happen to you? Will people laugh at you, take advantage of you, shun you? To the ego, love feels risky and unsafe. Much of what keeps people following their egos is a fear of what might happen if they stop doing what they've done in the past and what they see everyone else doing. The ego has a herd mentality.

There is a tremendous amount of peer pressure to do things the ego likes to do rather than to be virtuous. For instance, the ego loves to gossip. It's hard not to gossip when others are! The ego is vain and loves to preen and look good for every occasion, and that sets the standard for everyone. The ego accumulates money, power, and material things and looks down on those who don't have these things. Do you want to be looked down on? The ego judges, ostracizes, and even hates others for not believing, looking, or being like it. No one likes being judged. Judging keeps people in line, keeps people following the herd.

Make no mistake: Following the path of love and goodness takes courage. Those who are not choosing love don't like to be reminded that they aren't doing so. In their hearts, they know that love is the way, but they assume that no ordinary human being can live up to what I taught, and that's their excuse for not doing so or not even trying.

But I did not make myself superior to you; religion did this. I said, "Whoever believes in me (i.e. believes in love) will do the works I have been doing, and they will do even greater things than these." I taught love, with no excuses for your human nature. Yes, forgive yourself and others when you fail to live up to love, which you sometimes will, but don't give up trying to choose love instead of the ego. Don't give up on love just because love takes effort and, at times, you falter.

Faltering is part of the path of love. It is your intention to love and your willingness to put love first that sets this path apart from the path of the ego. No one follows love perfectly, but not trying is another story. Your intention is important—and your attention. What do you intend for your life and what are you giving your attention to? The answer to that question will tell you which path you are on.

I'm pointing this out for a reason: Many aren't really trying to follow what I taught. They aren't putting love first. This may be because they don't know what this looks like, since there are few models for this, or because they imagine that putting love first is too hard or unpleasant. When people hear someone talk about living a life dedicated to love, they often think of Mother Teresa, and if that's what the path of love looks like, most people don't want anything to do with it, understandably.

Do you see how the ego uses the example of Mother Teresa to discourage people from the path of love? A renunciate nun and missionary? That's the ego's worst nightmare: to be poor and powerless (and a woman) and to have renounced the pleasures of life. The implication is that the path of love is harsh, if not impossible for the average human being, and requires sacrifices you would never want to make.

The truth is, as I've been saying, the path of love rewards you with everything you have ever really wanted. It is also an easy path, not a difficult one, but you have to step onto it first, which is the hard part. To do that, you have to buck the crowd. Most of you on the spiritual path know what I'm talking about. You know how hard it is to be different from family members and others who can't relate to spiritual aspirations.

I'm not saying you have to retreat from the world or stop associating with others to tread the path of love, but your relationship to the world and others will need to change and will change. If you join with others in their conversations in the usual way, with gossip, complaints, judgments, self-righteousness, and unexamined opinions, nothing will change in your life or in the world. You won't change, and you won't be a force for love and change, but a maintainer of the egoic state of consciousness.

To be a changemaker, which is what the world needs—it needs more love—you have to be with others differently. You have to *not* do what the ego does when you're with others. Then, there will be room for love. If you fill your conversations with the usual talk, that's all there will be: egos talking to egos. This world doesn't need more of that; it needs more love. It needs you to stop doing what your ego does.

Let's examine the ego's usual contributions in conversation so that you can become more aware of what your ego sounds like and what it's up to. In general, what it's up to is trying to make you right and superior to others. Knowing this will make it easier to choose to not express the ego's viewpoint.

Judgments are one of the most obvious and common signs that your ego is speaking. All judgments come from the ego. If you stop believing and giving voice to your judgments, including judgments about others who aren't present, your relationships will be much improved. Key words that run through judgments are "should," "shouldn't," "should have," "could," and "could have," as in "He shouldn't have done that" or "She should be nicer."

The big lie, here, is that someone should or could be different than he or she is, or should have or could have behaved differently. This is a lie because most people are not in control of their behavior. They aren't consciously choosing to behave the way they do, but are being run by their programming. This deserves your compassion and understanding, not your disdain and judgment. You, too, are being run by your programming when you judge them, so be careful: "Judge not lest you be judged."

Judging is a vicious circle: You judge others, and then you feel bad about yourself because you've gone against love. Then, you judge some more in an attempt to further elevate yourself, but that only backfires and makes you feel worse. When people judge their loved ones or get together and judge others, they are digging themselves deeper and deeper into a hole of self-hatred, and the cycle continues.

This is essentially the story of the egoic state of consciousness: The ego's strategies for feeling better don't work. But that is as it's meant to be. Judging and other egoic strategies don't work because they are anti-love. Life is actually rigged against the ego and is pointing you back to love through suffering.

Judgments also often contain opinions and comparisons, such as "She isn't nearly as nice as he is." Egos love to compare one thing to another and one person to another. This has some value if you are picking out an apple at the grocery store, but comparing one *person* to another is pure ego.

Human beings are unique. Why compare anyone to another? Doing that is truly like comparing an apple to an orange. Such comparisons are the ego sizing itself and others up to see where it fits in the hierarchy in its own mind and trying to jockey for a higher position. This doesn't work because you'll always be able to find someone who is better than you in some way.

Comparing yourself to others is a favorite pastime of the ego, but you never come out on top for long. In this way, the ego keeps you tied to it through suffering. By keeping you in a contracted state, you are susceptible to further contraction, as you continue to turn to the ego for a way out of the contractions it has caused. The only way out is love, which means stop judging others and stop comparing yourself with others. Judgments and comparisons only take you deeper into the ego's lies and suffering.

The ego also likes to share its opinions with others, which can be useful if you are passing along helpful information. However, that is generally not what the ego does. The ego has another agenda, which is to make itself right and superior. For that, any opinion will do, because it's *how* this opinion is shared that creates the perception of being right and superior, and to the ego, perception is everything. In fact, most of the ego's opinions are not informed but guesses, prejudices, preferences, and unexamined conditioning. The ego pretends to know so much more than it actually does. Notice this, and you can become free of this tendency.

The ego shares its opinions, judgments, and other perceptions with great confidence and authority, like any good conman. People believe what the voice in their head says because it speaks with such confidence and authority. Then, pride keeps them in the egoic state of consciousness because they don't want to see that they don't really know much at all.

To be free from the ego, you have to be humble enough to admit that you don't know or that you were wrong: "Whoever exalts himself will be humbled, and he who humbles himself will be exalted." Humility is a quality of your divine nature. When you stop doing what the ego does—exalting yourself—and are willing to admit that you don't know very much at all, only then will you drop into the inner kingdom and experience the glory of your true nature.

I said something similar when I said, "Blessed are the meek, for they shall inherit the earth." Those who are gentle, unassuming, and do not seek power over others will be inwardly rich in this earthly dimension.

True riches are to be had when you stop doing what the ego does and live as I did, if only because life will be so much easier. Put love first: "Seek first the kingdom of heaven, and all else will be added unto you." When you put first things first, life becomes so much easier and happier, and likely more abundant.

Who is this *you* that the ego is trying to make superior? It's just an assortment of ideas about who you are. So much suffering and pain just to uphold an idea about yourself! This is wasted energy. How much happier and easier your life can be when you invest your energy in reality, in experiencing life just as it is, enjoying it, and flowing with it instead of arguing with it and bucking the river.

A river is the perfect metaphor for describing the difference between the ego's way of being and love's. Life is the river that carries you downstream, through all its twists and turns. As you travel down the river, you can like it or not, be happy or not, tell a sad story or not, be mad or not. The journey is still the same journey, but your experience of it will be very different depending on your internal state. You can also either paddle with the river or buck it and try to go upstream. That is your choice, and depending on what you choose, your experience will be very different.

You have been given free will. You can choose the ego's perceptions of not good enough and "I don't like," or your divine self's, which loves and embraces whatever is happening. You can be the happy traveler or the unhappy traveler. You are free to choose *how* you will be on the journey, but not taking the journey and not experiencing whatever is part of the journey is not an option.

How much better it is to accept the journey you are on. Your ego thinks it can shape the river and the journey to its liking, and that mistaken belief is the cause of much suffering. You have only so much control over the life you are given, but fortunately, something very wise and good is in control. When you see the truth—that life is the way it is and that it is a gift just as it is—then you can relax and enjoy the ride, even the rapids and the twists and turns.

On this journey, you'll discover that you've been given all the courage, strength, patience, and wisdom you need. And you are not alone on this journey. Many unseen helpers and friends are accompanying you as well.

When you see life through your divine self's eyes, life is divine, but when you see life through the ego's eyes, you suffer. Once you realize this, you are free to choose how you will perceive life. This is the gift of free will. Eventually, everyone comes to see life through the eyes of love.

You are being given the gift of the Truth now, so that must mean you are ready for it. All that's left is for you to exercise your free will to choose against the programming, against the path of least resistance. All that's left is for you to choose love in every moment as best you can.

So far, I have given you three things to look out for and give up to help you move out of the egoic state of consciousness: judgments, comparisons, and uninformed opinions. These include "shoulds," "should nots," "could haves," and "better than" and "less than." These words are warning flags that you are caught in the ego's perceptions.

Other words that trap you in the egoic state of consciousness are "I like," "I don't like," "I want," and "I don't want." These words indicate desires and preferences that keep you tied to the rollercoaster of feelings generated by the ego: If you're experiencing what you like or what you want, you're happy; if you aren't, you aren't happy.

Meanwhile, life is whatever it is, while the ego is labeling it good or bad, desirable or undesirable. Those labels determine whether you are happy going down the river or not. Without those labels, you're just having the experience of going down the river and responding to each twist and turn as it occurs, using all the God-given resources you have at your disposal.

With these few, very powerful words—"I like, I don't like, I want, I don't want"—all emotions are created. When life doesn't match your likes and wants, you feel sad, angry, unhappy, discontent, disappointed, jealous, envious, resentful, or fearful. If you didn't hold your preferences and desires as meaningful and important—if you didn't believe them—you would feel none of these feelings.

I'm not saying there's anything wrong with your desires or these feelings, and you aren't entirely in control of whether they arise or not. It is human to have desires and feelings like these because it's human to have an ego. However, your destiny as a human being is to transcend your ego and become a Christed, or enlightened, human being, which is someone who sees the truth about life and the truth about desires and feelings. The truth is that it's possible to have desires and feelings but not be had by them. It's even possible to get to a place where you're experiencing very few desires and negative feelings.

To become free of suffering, here is what you need to know: Your likes and wants keep you in a state of unnecessary suffering and at a distance from love, for you can't be experiencing the negative feelings that result from your desires *and* be experiencing love. These are two different states of consciousness: the egoic state and the kingdom of heaven.

To move into the state where love abides, you must see the truth about these thoughts: "I want," "I don't want, "I like," and "I don't like." The truth is that they are lies. They are made up. By whom? By the programming. They are what all human beings generally like and don't like, and want and don't want.

The problem is that your ego's desires are irrelevant to what Life, with a capital "L," wants. Life's desires—Thy will—trump your ego's will when these are in conflict. The way you discover what Life wants is by noticing what is coming out of the flow. Whatever *is,* is what Life wants, and happiness lies in desiring that, while suffering lies in desiring anything other than that.

Life is as it is. Sometimes you like it and sometimes you don't, but that doesn't change a thing. I can't say this enough, because it really seems to you that your desires matter, like they somehow have the power to change what *is*. But it's too late to change what *is*. I'm not saying you can't change something in the future by taking steps to do that. You can take steps to change things going forward, but you can't change what already is by not liking it and wanting it to be different. Your desires have no impact on the present moment except to make you discontent with it.

Forgive me, please, for repeating myself, but I do so because the programming is broken down through repetition. Human beings believe what they hear repeatedly, which is one of the reasons you believe what is in your head. The voice in your head and other people's voices in their heads have repeated things to you so often that you're convinced that these lies and half-truths are true.

So, bear with me, as I repeat something else: No one can do this work for you. Only you can neutralize the thoughts in your head by seeing their falseness and turning away from them, by choosing to give your attention to reality instead, to what you're actually experiencing here and now.

What is your body experiencing? What intuitions, motivations, and inspirations, if any, are arising? What are you moved to do or not do? Is it time to do something or time to rest and just be? The answers to these questions are easy enough to ascertain, but you have to want to look in this direction. You have to want to be present to life.

To get to this place, two things are necessary. First, you have to have fallen out of love with the voice in your head because you've seen how untrue and unhelpful it is and what it does to your life. Second, you have to have realized that the present moment is sweet and has the answers to how to live your life.

"The kingdom of heaven is spread upon the earth, and people do not see it." A life of beauty and delight is awaiting you if you but give your attention to the life you are given in this moment rather than to an imaginary life you wish you had. You will know when you have entered the kingdom of heaven when you feel this delight and the simple joy of just being.

The path of love requires that you practice doing the opposite of what the ego does. This often amounts to simply not doing something you usually do, such as complain. Every time you forgo the usual complaints, gossip, bragging, judging, and comparisons that the ego so readily engages in, the tendency to do these things is weakened.

Notice the desire to complain, gossip, brag, judge or whatever your ego especially likes doing and just say no. Instead of acting on it, don't. Then, notice what that's like to not have indulged in that. You just made your relationships and your life better. You just made it easier to love yourself and others and for others to love you.

What is it that can be aware, stop, and not do what you usually do? That is the *you* that is waking up from the egoic programming. You are waking up. You are becoming more aware, and that awareness can only lead to more and more awareness and awakeness. You are on your way to becoming a living master!

Once you step on the path of love, you are rewarded by love with every step you take, and taking those steps will become easier and easier. Once you stop behaving like the unloving ego and stop believing that's who you are, you'll discover how easy it is to love yourself and love life. What a wonderful discovery to realize that you are goodness incarnate! When you steadfastly walk this path, that is what you discover.

So, allow me to make some suggestions that will help you become more firmly established on this path. The first one is to replace complaints, desires, and anything else that steals your happiness with a practice of noticing what you're grateful for. The instruction I gave you earlier was to not do what the ego does. A practice of gratitude makes this much easier to do because it gives you something else to do in place of what you usually do.

For instance, if your ego wants to complain about having to walk the dog, remind yourself how grateful you are to be able to walk and how grateful you are to have time to walk or how good this is for you or how wonderful you'll feel afterwards or how happy your dog will be. Focus on what is good and positive about what *is* rather than on what you don't like or what you wish were different. You can always find things to appreciate about the present moment.

The ego is in the habit of focusing on its desires rather than on what is good and beautiful about the way things are here and now. It overlooks and takes for granted what it has and focuses on what it doesn't have, as if that is the key to happiness, when it's just the opposite.

There is always something to be happy about. The ego might argue with that, but the divine self is simply happy to be alive, to exist. That is enough, and existing truly is enough to be happy. Happiness is just a matter of lowering the bar!

When you sit very quietly and just experience your beingness, you will eventually feel the peace, joy, and contentment of your true self. These wonderful feelings are there, and they are always there. You can learn to bring these feelings to the forefront. The more time you spend being present, the more you will experience peace, love, and joy as your foreground and the complaining, discontent mind in the background.

Another suggestion for when you find yourself caught up in the ego is to breathe more deeply and slowly for a few minutes. This will shift your consciousness more easily than anything else. Please do not underestimate the power of breathing slowly and deeply to change you from the inside out. Doing this will help you see things more positively. So, if you're having difficulty with the gratitude practice, take a few slow, deep breaths first and then look around and count your blessings.

Look out onto the world with fresh eyes that are full of gratitude, which see beauty everywhere. Your divine self is in love with life and in love with seeing, hearing, feeling, and experiencing. The egoic state of consciousness dulls the experience of real life, but without the overlay of the ego's desires and unhappiness, real life is wondrous, beautiful, rich, vibrant, and alive.

Those of you who meditate know what I'm talking about. Those of you who don't will find out if you commit yourself to meditation over a period of time. There is a whole new world out there, a whole new way of experiencing the world awaiting you once you turn away from the imaginary *you* and begin experiencing life from your divine self's perspective.

Chapter 8

As a Man Thinketh, so Is He

Few wiser words have ever been spoken than these from Proverbs: "As a Man thinketh, so is he." Many live in a hell of their own making without realizing their responsibility in this. And because they don't realize this, they remain stuck. I will do my best in this chapter to help you see that this is unnecessary. Life can be challenging, but it need not be a hell.

Hell is supposedly a place of eternal torment. It is something you, your divine self, would never wish on anyone, but the ego might. Because the ego is devoid of love, it has no empathy and no remorse and no moral compass. Its only compass is its desires, and those get the ego into trouble. So, the ego has dreamed up a place—Hell—where it threatens to put people or put itself to keep itself in check. The ego uses fear to intimidate and manipulate others despite the fact that love works much better. But what does the ego know of love? It knows only fear.

Hell is a reflection of the ego, of the ego's hatred, self-hatred, selfishness, and intolerance. Hell is everyone's worst nightmare. It is absent of love, sympathy, compassion, and forgiveness, with no way out. It's what you get when you take love, compassion, and forgiveness out of the picture.

Fortunately, love, compassion, and forgiveness are very much a part of the picture of life on earth. And fortunately, your true nature is not at all like the ego. It's because you're not like the ego that Hell is your worst nightmare. A world or realm without love would be horrible indeed for beings, like yourselves, that are of love. The unhappiness, despair, and cruelty would be unbearable.

And yet, societies can devolve into a hell of sorts. When the ego is allowed to reign, that is what happens. What keeps the ego in check? Besides your true nature and inborn moral compass, which points you toward love, the ego keeps itself in check to some extent through the superego, which is an aspect of the ego that judges and punishes the ego with shame and guilt—an interesting development in human evolution!

Through negative self-talk, shaming, and self-hatred, you judge and punish yourself internally for your mistakes and the things your ego causes you to do: "You are so stupid! How could you do that?" or "You're getting nowhere spiritually" are the types of things you say to yourself. This is the superego. The superego is what believes in using punishment and cruelty to reform itself and others. The superego is no more evolved than the very primitive ego that gave birth to it.

The problem with shame is that it is neither the best deterrent to bad behavior nor the best teaching device. Shame is unloving and hurtful, and there's a price to pay for shame, and that is self-esteem. When you shame someone, as the ego does, that person feels bad about himself or herself and remains vulnerable to further ego manipulation. Shame keeps people in the egoic state of consciousness, in a state of negativity.

To truly reform and transform people, they need support in moving out of the egoic state of consciousness. The first thing they need is love and forgiveness from others. This makes it easier for them to forgive themselves and to connect with the love within themselves. Then, it will be impossible for them to behave badly.

This is why forgiveness is so important and such a valuable tool for personal and societal transformation. Forgiveness allows people to begin again anew and reconnect with their innate loving nature rather than stay stuck in the egoic state of consciousness because of guilt, shame, or low self-esteem. Once people are connected with the love of their true nature, they begin to love themselves, and then they'll behave lovingly toward others.

As a society, you must help people end the vicious cycle of self-hatred by forgiving them and giving them skills to improve themselves and become more loving. The first skill to offer them is meditation. Teach them to meditate. This is how people can most easily connect with their true nature and see the truth about the voice in their head. Once they're on this road, transformation is possible. No one is so wayward that they can't be uplifted by helping them connect with their innate loving nature. There *is* a solution to much of the crime and violence in society.

The other means of uplifting people is attending to their basic needs if those needs are not being met. Love them by giving them what they need to be healthy members of society. Do they need food? Give it to them. Do they need training or education? Give it to them. Do they need emotional healing or health care? Give it to them.

This is obvious, isn't it? If people are committing crimes because they lack the basic necessities of life, then society has failed them. Serving those in your society this way is just good policy and good for society. If you don't, you'll pay the price through crime, incarceration, unrest, and unhappiness.

"Whatsoever you do to the least of my brethren, you do to me" means whatever good or harm you do to another, you do to yourself. Others *are* you in another disguise. You take care of them because that is how you would want to be treated. You "love one another" without exceptions—because there are no exceptions: Everyone is God. Everyone is your very own self, your divine self, in disguise.

People are healed and uplifted by one thing: love. Society is improved only through love, not through punishment or unequal treatment. Love is generous of spirit, caring, and compassionate. Love is also just and wise. Love gives, and it is wise enough to give what is needed and no more. You are always being guided in your giving by your intuition, inner wisdom, and the good feeling of rightness.

The reason given for not giving to those in need is often that giving will spoil them or make them lazy or weak. It's true that giving inappropriately or giving too much to others can lead to dependency or lack of self-sufficiency. Unfortunately, that reasoning is too often just an excuse to be selfish and unconcerned about others. Be your "brother's keeper." "Do unto others as you would have them do unto you." Give—if only to ensure that you also will be given to in your time of need, in keeping with the law of karma.

When people do give, they discover that giving is its own reward, and they'll continue to give simply because it feels good. And why does giving feel good? Because it's the right thing to do. By all means, do what feels good, not in the sense of physical pleasures, but what feels good intrinsically. Love feels good, and this good feeling is part of your inner guidance system.

I said that it is impossible to love yourself if you believe that you are the ego and if you're behaving like the ego, since the ego behaves badly. When you begin to give more and love more, all this changes, because this is doing the opposite of what the ego does. The reward of giving is not only that you make others feel good, which you surely do, but that you make yourself feel good about yourself.

This last part is important: You make yourself feel good! You have the power to make yourself feel good and to do things that result in loving yourself. You have always had this power, but most people don't use it to their fullest. They're too busy making themselves feel bad, creating their living hell.

Just as life can be hell, life can also be heaven, depending on what you are thinking and believing. So, we return to the chapter's theme: "As a Man thinketh, so is he." And you could add: As a Man thinketh, so does he feel. Your thoughts cause you to be a certain way and feel a certain way. So, let's explore this further.

It all begins with a thought: A thought arises in your mind. You didn't put that thought there, you didn't call it up, you didn't choose it from lots of other thoughts; it just showed up unbidden. You had nothing to do with that. Where did that thought come from?

It came from your unconscious mind. Although the unconscious mind is mysterious, it isn't completely unknown territory. People have known about the unconscious mind for a long time. It's a storehouse. It stores memories and all sorts of information and conditioning you've gathered throughout this and all your other lifetimes. It also houses the collective unconscious, which stores impressions gained from humanity's history. And it stores the programming that is the ego.

But that's not all: The unconscious mind is also a porthole to the soul. What I mean by this is that the soul's lessons and the soul's plan, including one's personality, karma, talents, psychological issues, wounds, and proclivities from past lives, are part of the programming stored in the unconscious mind.

In short, the unconscious mind stores information from one's current life, past lives, and humanity's history as well as the soul's programming and the ego's programming. Just as your computer is programmed to perform specific tasks, you have programming that causes you to respond to life in habitual and programmed ways.

This is all to say that you are not in control of what thoughts arise from the unconscious mind and appear as the voice in your head. This is determined by forces beyond you, some of which are benevolent and some not, for there is one other aspect to the unconscious mind that must be mentioned: negative influence by nonphysical entities.

Just as those guiding you work with your unconscious mind to help and heal you, negative nonphysical entities can also influence you through your unconscious mind—if you are in a negative state. This is all the more reason to keep your thoughts as positive as possible, which I will say more about shortly.

I mention these negative entities because it's important that you understand that some of the most ugly, hateful, and violent thoughts you have come from beyond you and beyond your ego, from nonphysical entities who have lost their way and are divorced from love.

I hesitate to use the word "possessed" because it's so highly charged, but these negative entities can use the unconscious mind to cause people to do things that they would never do were it not for their influence. This influence is largely through the voice in the head, which arises from the unconscious mind.

These entities are not to be feared, as they are not powerful. But they cause many to hate themselves and even harm themselves and others. They are most certainly involved in most suicides and violent crimes and other sociopathic behavior. Eventually, these negative entities will "see the light," literally and figuratively, and return to love, as everyone does.

If this phenomenon were more widely understood, there would be more compassion for criminal behavior and better tools for dealing with it. As it stands, the negativity heaped by society on those influenced in this way makes this a real win for negative entities, who want nothing more than to promulgate fear and hatred in human society.

If you'd like to understand more about this phenomenon and how to work with such negativity, I refer you to this author's book *Getting Free: Moving Beyond Negativity and Limiting Beliefs*. The point I want to make here, now, is that your hateful and extremely negative thoughts are literally not yours. Your darkest thoughts are not coming from your ego but from beyond you. They're being planted in your unconscious mind by those who wish to manipulate you and wreak havoc in your world.

There's no reason to feel bad about having such thoughts, or even about the thoughts that come from your own ego. They mean nothing about you. Your true nature is love, and nothing these entities do can change that. As I said, these entities aren't powerful except if you believe them and do their bidding.

"As a Man thinketh, so is he" doesn't mean that you are bad if you have bad thoughts—everyone has bad thoughts. What this means is that the thoughts that you believe and act on determine how you see yourself, how others see you, and what you draw to you in life through karma and otherwise.

"As a Man thinketh" determines a person's sense of self and what results from that sense of self, but this sense of self has nothing to do with who you really are. Your divine self is never harmed or changed by anything you think or even do. Your thinking determines the false self's experience of life, not your true self's.

When you're lost in a negative sense of self and behaving badly, it's like the divine self is temporarily lost in a bad dream. Just as you, the dreamer, is untouched by what happens in your dreams, the divine self is untouched by the experience the illusory false self is having and allows that experience to play itself out. The divine self allows the false self to have whatever experience it is creating, knowing that valuable learning will be gained from that, at least eventually.

God allows all manner of experiences created by the ego and by negative entities who are lost to love because God is willing to have such experiences. As a means of exploration, God created a realm, such as yours, in which good and the appearance of evil exist. I say, "the appearance of evil" because there is no such thing as evil. Only love exists. Evil is what results from the absence of love, from someone becoming divorced from love.

That God would allow evil and even choose to experience it as a human being is very difficult for most to understand and accept. Nevertheless, this interplay of dark and light is just the way it is on earth and must be accepted. The best explanation for this is that compassion and deep devotion to love are developed by experiencing the opposite of these. The value of love is realized by experiencing its opposite.

You are fortunate to be encountering this teaching now, because once you see the truth about love and its importance, you no longer have to be at the effect of negativity. If you don't believe the voice in your head's thoughts, you can't be affected by those thoughts. To the extent that you've seen the truth about negativity, you have transcended duality: the perception of good and evil.

Here is the truth about negativity: The negativity in your egoic mind is never true. The negative pole is a mirage. All there is, is love: positivity. The negative pole is simply the absence or near absence of love, just as darkness is the absence of light.

The negative pole is created by the egoic programming and reinforced by negative nonphysical entities, who don't believe in love. They are lost to love only because they've believed others who've told them that love doesn't exist. They've been told that if they go toward the Light, where they will experience love, they will perish. They believe that love is deadly.

Negative nonphysical entities believe the opposite of the truth, so that becomes their reality. The same is true for you: If you believe the opposite of the truth, then that becomes your reality: "As a Man thinketh, so is he." Reality conspires to prove to you what you believe to be true.

To negative entities, it really seems like love doesn't exist and that what is termed love is dangerous, because they are associating only with those who believe this and who, consequently, behave horrifically toward each other. These negative entities are living in a hell realm of their own creation because of what they believe. This happens to human beings as well.

Fortunately, once negativity is no longer believed, it stops existing as part of your reality because it's been seen for what it is: a deep misunderstanding. Once a lie is seen as a lie, it can't be believed anymore, and then it stops being a force in your life.

What remains in your mind when negativity has departed or is no longer given any weight is Truth: love. The truth is positive. Life is essentially and inherently good, benevolent, and of love. This is wonderful news!

How many are not aware of this? How many are living in the ego's illusory world and perceiving life through their ego's eyes? Unfortunately, most people. But that is not your fate, and it isn't anyone's ultimate fate, for everyone will see the truth about life at some point.

Now that you've seen the truth, what will you do about it? Unfortunately, you won't be released from negativity the instant you see the truth about it. Becoming free of the ego is a process. You have to see through the negative thoughts one by one as they arise.

This means you have to become aware of what you're thinking moment to moment. You have to be very committed to seeing this, or your negative thoughts can still trip you up. But as you see these thoughts for what they are—useless lies—they will weaken and show up in your mind less frequently. Eventually, many of them will drop away forever. Your mind will become more spacious, quiet, and more positive. This is the process.

The first step is to learn to become aware of your thoughts. This awareness is what is developed in meditation. The second step is to question your thoughts, especially your "I" thoughts and any that are negative or limiting. Ask yourself, "Is that true?"

The answer is always no, but can you see this clearly? The reason these thoughts aren't true is that they don't contain the whole truth. They leave out so much, and they aren't *always* true. Something that is true is the whole truth and always true.

An example of a true statement is "Love is behind life." This statement is always true but not something the voice in your head would tell you. You might tell it to yourself to quiet the voice in your head, but the voice in your head won't be what comes up with such a truth.

If you apply this standard to your thoughts—that, to be true, they must be true always, throughout time—it will become obvious that nearly all your thoughts are not true. Most are neither universal truths nor facts, but assumptions, beliefs, fantasies, desires, faulty memories, fears about an unknown future, stories that tell only part of the story, incomplete characterizations of yourself, and out-and-out fabrications.

The voice in your head is the spinner of the Illusion that is the cause of all suffering, what Hindus and Buddhists call *maya*. The illusion it is spinning is the negative pole. The negative pole is created by the voice in your head. Without the voice in your head, all that remains is Truth, with a capital "T," and facts.

Facts are neutral and can't cause suffering unless you spin a story about them that makes you suffer. And Truth is always positive: Life is good, love is behind life, suffering is a great teacher, there is a way out of suffering, you are eternal, life is a school, everyone is always learning and evolving, people are essentially good and loving, you have all of the inner resources you need to be happy, happiness is here right now. I could go on.

These are immutable truths. Look at the thoughts in your egoic mind, and you won't find these kinds of thoughts. What you will find is thoughts that cause suffering, thoughts that don't serve you—thoughts that are, in fact, not true.

"The Truth will set you free," while what is false will imprison you—and that is exactly what happens. The lies and half-truths your egoic mind tells you imprison you and keep you in a state of suffering, confusion, and discontentment. But there is something outside those prison walls, and that is good news. There is Truth, there is love, there is freedom from suffering. I am so happy you are discovering this, and it brings me joy to support you in seeing the Truth. Welcome to my world, where there is only love.

Once you've seen that a thought isn't true, it will stop being of interest to you. Like a magic trick that you've seen through, those thoughts will no longer captivate, frighten, or motivate you. Then, it will be easy to give your attention to something that *is* true: real life.

Once you really see that your mind has nothing to offer you—no good advice, wisdom, guidance, insights, or even entertainment—you'll be more willing to turn to the present moment for satisfaction, and you'll find it there. The more satisfaction you find in the present moment, the more you'll choose to stay there, and the more you stay there, the more that becomes your established way of being.

"As a Man thinketh, so is he" is not only a basic truth, but also a formula for speeding up the process of freeing yourself from the voice in your head. Since what you think affects how you feel and what you experience and become, you can choose to think thoughts that will help you become who you are meant to be: your divine self. You are meant to be an expression of goodness, of God, in the world!

What is it that can choose to turn away from a thought or think a thought? That is your divine self, your true self. While you don't choose the thoughts that appear in your mind as the voice in your head, you can choose to not believe those thoughts and you can choose to think thoughts that are true instead.

When the divine self is awake enough within you, it begins to counteract the egoic programming and other false conditioning with the truth. The truth is received by you intuitively, and then you, as your divine self, choose to affirm it and focus on it mentally or repeat it out loud to yourself. This is how the unconscious mind is reprogrammed and the voice in your head quieted. Before one awakens, some reprogramming of this nature is often necessary.

By replacing negative thoughts from the unconscious mind with true statements, the negative thoughts are healed or uprooted. Some will never resurface again, while others will be so weak when they do surface that they can easily be ignored.

This is essentially what happens when people awaken: They realize the truth about life on a deep level, and this wipes out many of their mistaken beliefs. Over time, the rest fall away one by one. The Truth becomes so apparent that they can no longer be fooled by the voice in their head, at least not for long. The result is that this voice falls into the background and is easily ignored. What they are left with is the present moment's love, peace, wisdom, and delight.

People who've had lengthy and deep experiences of the present moment don't want to return to the suffering of their old way of being—and they can't. Once you've seen through all the magic tricks, you stop going to the magic show for entertainment. You've discovered a whole new way of being that has made the old way obsolete.

This new way of being feels magical, delightful, vibrant, alive, beautiful, wondrous, sparkly. All these words are attempts to describe the state of presence, the domain of your divine self—the kingdom of heaven—when it's being experienced deeply. This is the state young children experience when they're lost in play. Walt Disney, in much of his animation, captured the beauty, vibrancy, goodness, love of life, gratitude, and joy of this state, which is why his creations are so beloved.

This beauty and goodness is what people want and what they know to be true on a deep level. When you've fallen deeply enough into reality, you see that the beauty and goodness of the world depicted in Disney's animation is not a fantasy.

One of the best tools for gaining the kingdom of heaven is reprogramming the unconscious mind, which is really quite programmable. The method is repetition. Whatever you repeatedly think to yourself is reinforced and felt to be true. If you repeat a positive statement to yourself often enough, then that will become what is true to you.

Doing this will make your mind less negative and less compelling, which is the goal. Although you may never eliminate all negativity, neutralizing much of it and weakening the rest is enough to make it possible to stay in presence longer and eventually live in presence.

Some people's unconscious minds are clearer than others from the start. They were born with a lighter load of negativity and fewer misunderstandings from previous lifetimes, so they have less work to do to become free of them. Whatever the state of your unconscious mind is, doing the work to free yourself from it is essential to the path of love and, in any event, must be done.

Clearing the unconscious mind is a matter of:

❖ Seeing the truth about a mistaken belief,

❖ Refusing to reinforce it by not dwelling on it or acting on it,

- ❖ Counteracting or neutralizing that belief by telling yourself some true statements that allow you to relax and be at peace, and

- ❖ Turning your attention to your sensory experience in the here and now.

Let me give you an example. You have the thought: "I won't be able to support myself." Any number of statements could be used to counteract or neutralize this thought. Here are a few:

I don't know that.

All is well and unfolding as it needs to.

"Look at the birds of the air, for they neither sow nor reap nor gather into barns; yet your heavenly Father feeds them."

Life is supportive and good.

One day at a time.

I'll cross that bridge when I come to it.

Be at peace.

I am the beloved son/daughter of a loving and generous Father.

I have always been supported one way or another.

I'll let tomorrow take care of that.
It'll be okay.

As you can see, quite a range of thoughts can neutralize the thought, "I won't be able to support myself." Any of the statements above will calm the limbic system, which is responsible for stress and the fight or flight response. When you aren't actually running from tigers, fight or flight is a dysfunctional state. Unfortunately, even a fearful thought can put you into this dysfunctional state.

Almost any positive statement you come up with will calm the limbic system and be helpful. The specific words you use are not that important. More important is your intention to overcome negativity. Every time you make an effort to overcome the ego, spiritual forces come forward to support and assist you. They are always there, encouraging and supporting you in moving in the direction of love, joy, and freedom, and your intention draws them to you.

Another reason that almost any positive statement will do is that any statement will keep you from dwelling on the negative thought. By stopping and finding a positive thought to replace the negative one, you've interrupted that negative thought and undermined its power to determine your state of consciousness.

The value of doing this work is obvious: You won't fall into a negative state. But also, if you can maintain a positive state, you'll have access to your divine self's guidance and wisdom. This is crucial and perhaps the most important reason for distancing yourself from negative thoughts. They don't serve you *and* they undermine your ability to be in touch with the life that is living you, which knows exactly how to support you in your life lessons and life purpose.

Life is supportive. Why would it create you and then not support you? If you have a lesson to learn about supporting yourself, you may experience difficulties; but even then, you'll be given all the support you need within yourself and from others to learn this lesson. If no lesson is involved, then Life will naturally support you as you travel your path.

However, if you're not on the path that Life wants you on, Life may try to steer you away from whatever path you're on by not supporting you on that path. This is a loving act. It is Life's job to keep you in line with your soul's plan. If your situation supports your lessons and plan, then there's no need for Life to do anything but support you in that situation. If you follow your Heart—your internal guidance system—Life will surely support you. There is no reason that it wouldn't.

Chapter 9

Conclusion

One of the most honest things you can say is "I love." It is the Truth, with a capital "T." Just stop a moment right now and say this to yourself and notice how that feels, just those two words with nothing after them.

Many times a day, you say "I love" something or someone, but that's often the ego speaking: "I love that color," "I love ice cream," "I love doing that." There's nothing wrong with such statements, of course, and they may even be expressions from your divine self, but these statements don't feel the same as saying "I love." There's a big difference between giving voice to a preference and speaking the Truth, and this can be felt subtly, energetically, inside yourself. These represent two different states of consciousness.

The simple statements "I love" and "I am love," which are rarely spoken, are two of the most powerful things you can say. If you give your full attention to them as you say them, they'll bring you into alignment with your divine self. Because of that, either of these phrases can be used as a mantra.

A mantra is a word or phrase that brings people into presence when chanted or repeated mentally. Usually, the word or phrase has some sacred meaning, but your intention for doing this is what is most important. If you hold any word or phrase as sacred and intend that it bring you into presence, it will if you repeat it often enough. Repeating a mantra focuses the mind and keeps you from getting lost in egoic thoughts. The natural result is that you become present.

I hope you will try out "I love" and "I am love" as mantras by repeating them silently to yourself for ten minutes or so a day. Just doing this can make a real difference in your life. It's a way of reprogramming your mind and erasing some of the limiting and untrue "I" statements that are behind any negative sense of self.

The false self is made up of the "I" statements that you believe and give voice to. The ones that you deeply believe shape your behavior in ways you may not be aware of. By neutralizing some of those "I" statements with "I love" or "I am love" or some other statement of Truth, your sense of self and inner state will change and, consequently, your behavior. You'll become different: "As a Man thinketh, so is he." "I" and "I am" statements drive and shape your life because they determine how you see yourself, how you feel, and what you do and say.

You may not feel you're in control of your ego's "I" thoughts, and as I have said, you aren't in control of what "I" thoughts arise in your mind, but you do have some control over whether you believe them or not. What you've believed about yourself in the past will arise again and again in your mind, because that's how programming works. Your programming is held in place and reinforced by believing it, and that won't change until you stop believing it.

Try replacing your "I" and "I am" thoughts with "I love" and "I am love." Nothing has to change in your speech with others. I'm only suggesting you replace your "I" and "I am" *thoughts* with "I love" and "I am love." Even doing this occasionally, like when you find yourself caught in negativity, will go a long way toward reprogramming your mind.

This will become easier and more natural as you practice this. More and more, you will find yourself remembering to do this. You'll stop yourself from thinking about yourself in the usual ways and replace that with thinking of yourself as love and as loving, and therefore as lovable. That is the reward for doing this work: You'll love yourself.

Love is fulfilling because it is your nature to love. When a bird flies or sings, that fulfills the bird because its nature is to fly and to sing. The same is true for you: When you love, you are fulfilled because it is your nature to love. So, if you prevent yourself from expressing love or do anything counter to love, you won't be fulfilled. In fact, you will hurt.

Such is the human condition. Human beings hurt because they stop themselves from being loving or do things that are unloving. They go against their true nature. When you do that, feeling bad is the right experience, because going against your true nature isn't meant to feel good.

Life is very kind this way in leading you back to love with a "stick." Life will use a "carrot" when it can, but sometimes a stick is necessary to get someone's attention. In this way, Life shows you what works in life and what doesn't, what is true and what isn't. When you are true to the Truth, you don't suffer; when you are not true to the Truth, you do. This is how you know what is true and what is not true.

The Truth is easy to follow because following it feels good. Misunderstandings are the only things keeping people from following love more often. Your programming causes you to misunderstand life. But, thankfully, there is a cure for that, which is love.

Life is this journey toward correcting these misunderstandings and discovering the Truth, in a world where nearly everyone is blind to it. Your world is built on misunderstandings, but humanity will find its way. As was true when I was alive, love is the way, and it is the only way. That is the only dogma I have to offer you. Go toward love, be love, love your neighbor as yourself, and be at peace. I am with you always.

About the Author

Gina Lake is a nondual spiritual teacher and the author of more than twenty books about awakening to one's true nature. She is also a gifted intuitive and channel with a master's degree in Counseling Psychology and over thirty years' experience supporting people in their spiritual growth. In 2012, Jesus began dictating books through her. These teachings from Jesus are based on universal truth, not on any religion.

Then in 2017, at the request of Jesus, Gina and her husband, who is also a nondual spiritual teacher, began offering Christ Consciousness Transmissions to groups online in weekly meetings and monthly intensives. These energy transmissions are a direct current of love and healing that accelerate one's spiritual evolution.

Gina's YouTube channel has over 250 messages from Jesus to listen to. Her website offers information about her books, online courses, transmissions, a free ebook, and audio and video recordings:

www.RadicalHappiness.com

If you enjoyed Awakening Love *and are looking for more specific guidance about relationships, we think you will find this book by Gina Lake enlightening:*

Choosing Love

Moving from Ego to Essence in Relationships

Here is an excerpt from this book:

What Not to Do with Anger

Once anger is there, you can't make it go away. You are stuck with it, but only momentarily if you know how to handle it. If you don't feed it by telling a story, it will just disappear. Anger gets out of hand because we try to support and defend it with a story. We feel uncomfortable about being angry, so we make up a story to justify our anger, and this story intensifies our feelings. This story often has little to do with the conditioning that triggered the anger.

For example, you hear kids making noise as they play outside in the street, and this triggers your conditioning: "Kids shouldn't play in the street." (Another "should" statement.) This view seems true to you, although many kids and even their parents would disagree, so you feel angry and self-righteous. However, the amount of anger you feel seems out of proportion to the situation, so you have to tell a story to justify the intensity of your feelings: "Last year, when they played ball in the street, they broke the Smith's window."

The trouble is that telling this story makes you feel even angrier and more justified in your anger. You stew about this story a little longer and come up with a few more reasons why kids shouldn't play in the street. Your mind searches for examples in the past and reaches for reasons why kids playing in the street would be bad in the future, and you conclude something out of proportion to the original thought: "I've got to move out of this neighborhood!" Now kids are to blame for your having to move. Anger—or really the stories we tell and the conclusions we come to—causes us a lot of trouble, and this is doubly true in relationships.

Telling stories to justify your anger and drumming up more reasons to be angry is definitely not the way to deal with anger, unless you like being angry and fighting. But it does give the ego some degree of pleasure, which is why we do it.

Exercise: Noticing How the Ego Enjoys Finding Fault

It's useful to notice the enjoyment the ego gets from finding fault and picking a fight. Most of all, it's useful to notice that it is the ego that is doing this, and you are not the ego. That means you don't have to find fault. Doing so is a choice, and you can choose to do something else.

Whether you are telling stories to justify the anger, drumming up more reasons to be angry, going back over past incidents that made you angry, or thinking about what might make you angry in the future, thinking about anything related to the conditioning and the anger is just not helpful. Nevertheless, this is exactly what the ego does. As a way of sustaining the conditioning, the ego often mentally repeats it: "You shouldn't leave your dishes in the sink. You just shouldn't do it. How can someone do that? It's just not right." In the same way, the ego sustains the anger by repeatedly going over its stories about it and justifications for it: "He's an inconsiderate slob. He's always been a slob. His mother was a slob. I would never do that to him. He just doesn't care about me. Maybe he never cared. I don't think he loves me. He's too much of a slob for me. He's not considerate enough for me. Maybe I don't love him." In a few short minutes, the internal dialogue has gone from being annoyed at dishes in the sink to considering divorce. Anger causes us to lose touch with our love for someone. It also kills the desire for sex with that person.

Thinking is what holds the ego in place and keeps the conditioning, feelings, and unhappiness going. It creates and maintains problems. It's a real troublemaker. Choosing to believe thoughts is choosing to be identified with the ego, and it's possible to make another choice.

Another thing that doesn't help in dealing with anger is blaming yourself for it or for the conditioning that caused it. Taking anger personally (by assuming blame for it) makes you feel bad about yourself and will only take you deeper into the anger because you'll feel like you have to justify it. And justifying your anger will only create more anger and more bad feelings about yourself.

You don't need to justify your anger or defend your conditioning because they are not yours. They don't belong to you—to the real you—but to the false self. You are only responsible for what you do with your feelings once they are there.

Just as it's not helpful to blame yourself for your anger, it's not helpful to blame others for theirs either. The ego's strategy for feeling better about being angry is to make up stories to justify it and to blame others for it. This just creates more anger and bad feelings all around. By blaming someone else, we involve another person, who also has an ego and its own conditioning, judgments, and bad feelings. And that's just more trouble.

Contrary to common belief, it is also not helpful to share your anger with your partner. The general assumption about anger is that if we don't do something about it or talk about it, we aren't dealing with it. But, unfortunately, most of what we say or do about our anger is destructive to relationships. You may think that telling your partner when you're angry is healthy, but that's a misconception. It's far better to notice the anger, take responsibility for it, and not dump it on, or even try to process it with, your partner, because doing so doesn't serve the anger or the relationship.

Here's an example of what might happen when you tell your partner you are angry at her for throwing out something you needed. You might say something like this:

> *I can't believe you threw out that paper. Now I don't know who to call about this. You always do that. I wish you wouldn't straighten up my desk and papers. You could at least ask me before throwing something away. You're so compulsive. You really need to look at that.*

This may seem like a perfectly reasonable response to this situation. However, the truth is that the paper is gone, and any discussion about it isn't going to change that. And your partner's future behavior isn't likely to change either if you alienate him or her with your criticism. More likely, it will trigger your partner's ego and defensiveness:

I just couldn't stand the mess anymore. You should clean up your desk. You know it bothers me when it's messy. I can't help it. I needed to clean under those papers. If I left it up to you, it would be filthy in here – and you wouldn't even care!

At this point, your partner isn't any closer to cooperating with you in the future, and now you both feel angry. And nothing has changed. The paper is still gone. Is your anger worth it? Is being right worth it? Is punishing each other with angry words worth it?

Keeping the anger to yourself is not the same thing as repressing it, which is denying that it's there or being unaware that it's there. You acknowledge that it's there, but you keep it to yourself. The reason for this advice is twofold: First, by keeping it to yourself, you are not as likely to dwell on it and feed it with stories to try to convince your partner of your position. Second, by keeping it to yourself, you avoid the possibility of triggering your partner's conditioning and a potentially unproductive or destructive interaction.

Discussions about conditioning aren't helpful if you and your partner are identified with the ego because they're bound to turn into arguments, which are destructive to a relationship. From this level, little can be accomplished. In discussing conditioning with your partner, the best that can be hoped for is that you come to understand each other's conditioning, but unless you both are identified with Essence when you are doing it, exploring conditioning isn't likely to be productive.

Even trying to do this from Essence has its limitations and dangers. Although your intent may be to explore and understand conditioning and not blame or judge your partner, your conditioning may get triggered by this discussion, and it may turn into an argument or at least become unproductive.

There's also no guarantee that the insights you come up with will be that useful or applied when the going gets tough. These insights can just as easily be discovered independently by meditating on the issue and asking for internal guidance. You don't need to get insight about your conditioning or your partner's from your partner. You can get it from yourself, and it's much safer to get it that way.

The same is true about processing your conditioning. If this is done at all, it's better to do it by yourself than with your partner, who has his or her own issues and points of view, which may not be that helpful to your understanding and healing. A therapist may be valuable, but don't make the mistake of thinking that your partner can or should be able to be your therapist. The ego is very tricky, and even couples with very pure intentions, a good grasp of psychology, and good communication skills can get sidetracked into blame, judgment, anger, and irrationality because the ego can be triggered at any time.

For more information about this book, go here:
https://RadicalHappiness.com/Choosing-Love

Christ Consciousness Transmission (CCT) Online Weekly Meetings

Transmission is something that naturally happens from spiritual teacher to aspirant and from beings on higher dimensions to those who are willing to receive on this dimension. Transmission has been used throughout the ages to accelerate spiritual evolution and raise consciousness. In the process, emotional and sometimes physical healing also take place, as a clearing of energy blocks from the energy field is a necessary and natural part of raising consciousness.

In weekly online Zoom video meetings, Gina Lake and her husband offer Christ Consciousness transmissions. This is one of the ways that Jesus and the other Ascended Masters working with Jesus intend to raise humanity's level of consciousness. A channeled message from Jesus is given before the transmission to prepare, teach, and inspire those who are there to receive the transmission. Many report feeling a transmission come through these channeled messages as well.

The transmission takes around twenty minutes and is done in silence except for some music, which is meant to help people open and receive. During the transmission, Gina Lake and her husband are simply acting as antennas for Christ Consciousness, as it streams to earth to be received by all who are willing to open to and be uplifted by divine grace. Since there is actually no such thing as time and space, these are not a barrier to receiving the transmission, which works as well online as in person. You can find out more about these transmissions on Gina's website at:

www.RadicalHappiness.com/transmissions

Awakening Now Online Course

It's time to start living what you've been reading about. Are you interested in delving more deeply into the teachings in Gina Lake's books, receiving ongoing support for waking up, and experiencing the power of Christ Consciousness transmissions? You'll find that and much more in the Awakening Now online course:

This course was created for your awakening. The methods presented are powerful companions on the path to enlightenment and true happiness. Awakening Now will help you experience life through fresh eyes and discover the delight of truly being alive. This 100-day inner workout is packed with both time-honored and original practices that will pull the rug out from under your ego and wake you up. You'll immerse yourself in materials, practices, guided meditations, and inquiries that will transform your consciousness. And in video webinars, you'll receive transmissions of Christ Consciousness. These transmissions are a direct current of love and healing that will accelerate your evolution and help you break through to a new level of being. By the end of 100 days, you will have developed new habits and ways of being that will result in being more richly alive and present and greater joy and equanimity.

www.RadicalHappiness.com/online-courses

More Books by Gina Lake

Available in paperback, ebook, and audiobook formats.

A Heroic Life: New Teachings from Jesus on the Human Journey. The hero's journey—this human life—is a search for the greatest treasure of all: the gifts of your true nature. These gifts are your birthright, but they have been hidden from you, kept from you by the dragon: the ego. These gifts are the wisdom, love, peace, courage, strength, and joy that reside at your core. *A Heroic Life* shows you how to overcome the ego's false beliefs and face the ego's fears. It provides you with both a perspective and a map to help you successfully and happily navigate life's challenges and live heroically. This book is another in a series of books dictated to Gina Lake by Jesus.

Jesus Speaking Series: In this series of four channeled audiobooks/books by Jesus, narrated by Gina Lake, Jesus speaks to us from another dimension to awaken Christ Consciousness within us. In this series, Jesus shows us how we can become more Christ-like and live as he did. These are nondual (Oneness) teachings and not based on any religion. Jesus explains:

> *"I am speaking to you now through this channel to help you to know of my presence and feel my presence in your life more fully. My intention is to help you realize your true nature and to live as the best human being you can be. Allow me to be your guide back home to love."*

What Jesus Wants You to Know Today: About Himself, Christianity, God, the World, and Being Human: Jesus exists and has always existed to serve humanity, and one way he is doing this today is through this channel, Gina Lake, and others. In *What Jesus Wants You to Know Today,* Jesus answers many questions about his life and teachings and shares his perspective on the world. He brings his message of love, once again, to the world and corrects the record by detailing the ways that Christianity has distorted his teachings. He wants you to know that you, too, have the potential to be a Christ, to be enlightened as he was, and he explains how this is possible.

From Stress to Stillness: Tools for Inner Peace. Most stress is created by how we think about things. *From Stress to Stillness* will help you to examine what you are thinking and change your relationship to your thoughts so that they no longer result in stress. Drawing from the wisdom traditions, psychology, New Thought, and the author's own experience as a spiritual teacher and counselor, *From Stress to Stillness* offers many practices and suggestions that will lead to greater peace and equanimity, even in a busy and stress-filled world.

In the World but Not of It: New Teachings from Jesus on Embodying the Divine: From the Introduction, by Jesus: "What I have come to teach now is that you can embody love, as I did. You can learn to embody all that is good within you. I came to show you the beauty of your own soul and what is possible as a human. I came to show you that it is possible to be both human and divine, to be love incarnate. You walk with one foot in the world of form and another in the Formless. This mysterious duality within your being is what this book is about." This book is another in a series of books dictated to Gina Lake by Jesus.

All Grace: New Teachings from Jesus on the Truth About Life. Grace is the mysterious and unseen movement of God upon creation, which is motivated by love and indistinct from love. *All Grace* was given to Gina Lake by Jesus and represents his wisdom and understanding of life. It is about the magnificent and incomprehensible force behind life, which created life, sustains it, and operates within it as you and me and all of creation. *All Grace* is full of profound and life-changing truth.

Awakening Love: How to Love Your Neighbor as Yourself: "This book is what I would teach about love if I were walking among you today. It takes its organization from particular quotes of mine and others from the Bible, which have come down through time. The quotes this book is built upon are the core teachings I gave then and I offer you today. If they are adhered to, they will change your life and change your world." –Jesus

The Jesus Trilogy. In this trilogy by Jesus, are three jewels, each shining in its own way and illuminating the same truth: You are not only human but divine, and you are meant to flourish and love one another. In words that are for today, Jesus speaks intimately and directly to the reader of the secrets to peace, love, and happiness. He explains the deepest of all mysteries: who you are and how you can live as he taught long ago. The three books in *The Jesus Trilogy* were dictated to Gina Lake by Jesus and include *Choice and Will, Love and Surrender,* and *Beliefs, Emotions, and the Creation of Reality.* Each of the books in the trilogy is also available individually and can be read in any order.

Faith, Facts, and Fiction: Finding Your Way on the Spiritual Path. In this channeled book by Jesus, he explains the ways people fool themselves and are fooled on the spiritual path and corrects many of the misunderstandings that many seekers have. How do you sort fact from fiction, faith from blind faith, and Truth from illusion? What's the truth about conspiracy theories, cults, Christianity, channeling, psychic abilities, awakening, and enlightenment? The answers are here.

Cycles of the Soul: Life, Death, and Beyond. What is the soul? And what is this human life all about? What happens at death and after death? What is it like in the afterlife, and do you plan your life before you are born? In this channeled book from Jesus, he answers these and many other questions. This wise and compassionate perspective from Jesus will help you embrace life and be at peace with life and with death.

Choosing Love: Moving from Ego to Essence in Relationships. Having a truly meaningful relationship requires choosing love over your conditioning: your ideas, fantasies, desires, images, and beliefs. *Choosing Love* describes how to move beyond judgment, anger, romantic illusions, and differences to love and oneness with another. It explains how to drop into your Being, where Oneness and love exist, and be with others from there.

For more information, please visit the "Books" page at
www.RadicalHappiness.com

Printed in Great Britain
by Amazon